Opening the Bidding

Improving Your Judgment

Audrey Grant

B_B

THE IMPROVING YOUR JUDGMENT SERIES

This series of mini-books introduces ideas and concepts that can improve your game. It brings you the latest theories from the world's greatest players. There's no better way to bring your game into the 21st century.

ISBN 0-9686547-0-3

Printed and bound in Canada

3 4 5 6 7   WC   04 03 02 01 00

Table of Contents

Acknowledgements

To my husband, David Lindop, a world-class player, who works hand-in-hand with me in all my bridge endeavors.

To the world-class players who have generously shared the secrets of the game.

To the bridge teachers. Your dedication, skill, and professionalism have made me proud to be counted among you.

Preface

If you're reading this book, you're likely an active, involved person . . . looking for adventure and searching for ways to improve your bridge game! A close look at the first bid and the impact it has on the entire auction is a good place to start.

The best theorists in the world have shared their secrets with me, and I bring these pieces of bridge wisdom to you in a manner which I hope you'll find readable. The material in this book can improve your opening bids . . . but the concepts will spread and help you improve your judgment in all aspects of the game.

Bidding conversations are effective when they are simple, yet accurate. Both partners have to be comfortable during the auction. The goal is to experience the excitement of the bidding conversation without the stress. I've often said that I don't want a point or two to come between friends. I hope you'll feel the same way after reading this book.

Congratulations for being interested in an activity that is a wonderful life skill and a way to spend time with friends whether they're in your neighborhood or from another part of the world.

All the very best,

Audrey Grant

HOW MANY PLAY A
16-18 NOTRUMP RANGE?

HOW MANY PLAY A
15-17 NOTRUMP RANGE?

THERE IS ONLY ONE
RIGHT ANSWER!

PLAY WITH SOMEONE
WHO HAD HIS HAND
RAISED AT THE SAME
TIME YOU DID.

Chapter One

Opening at the One Level —
In First and Second Position

The serve, the opening move in a chess game, the first bid in an auction, can all create the drama associated with making the first move. There are a number of guidelines to help make a good decision when you're given the chance to open the bidding. The focus of this book.is to provide tips for improving your judgement when you are in this important position.

You're the dealer. What's your call? The first step is to estimate the worth of your hand. There are two features to take into consideration: the high cards and the shape, or distribution. There is general agreement about the value of high cards. An Ace is worth 4 points, a King 3 points, a Queen 2 points, and a Jack 1 point.

Assessing the value of distribution is more controversial. It used to be that opener would value shortness by giving a void 3 points, a singleton 2 points, and a doubleton 1 point. Most experts now suggest that length is a better measure of the worth of a hand until a trump fit has been found. Instead of points for shortness, add one point for each card beyond four in a suit. A five-card suit is worth 1 point, a six-card suit 2 points, and so on.

Very unbalanced hands are usually evaluated by their trick-taking potential instead of their point count. If you held all thirteen spades, for example, the value would be far more than 10 high-card points plus 9 length points since you could take all the tricks if spades were trump.

In this chapter, you'll see how to use the *Rule of 20* and other guidelines to evaluate borderline hands when you have to decide whether to open the bidding at the one level.

Think of opener as the describer and responder as the decider—the decision maker. Your objective as opener is to give as clear a picture of your hand as you can in one bid.

Opening 1NT

An opening bid of 1NT paints the most specific picture of your distribution and strength.

Distribution

A notrump opening bid shows a *balanced hand*—a hand with no voids, no singletons, and no more than one doubleton. There are three hand patterns that fit this description:

x x x x	x x x x	x x x x x
x x x	x x x x	x x x
x x x	x x x	x x x
x x x	x x	x x
4-3-3-3	4-4-3-2	5-3-3-2

You don't need high cards in every suit, even if you have a doubleton. The five-card suit can be a major when you have 5-3-3-2 distribution. You can open 1NT with a *semi-balanced hand*—a hand with more than one doubleton—if opening the long suit might leave you awkwardly placed for a rebid. For example:

♠ Q 5
♥ K J
♦ K J 7 3
♣ K Q 8 4 2

If you open 1♣ and partner responds 1♥ or 1♠, a rebid of 1NT or 2♣ would show a minimum-strength hand. A rebid of 2♦ . . . a reverse . . . would show a hand of 17 or more points. By opening 1NT, you avoid any rebid problems.

Strength

The strength required for a 1NT opening bid is limited to a narrow three-point range. The most popular ranges in North America are 15-17 and 16-18. We're going to work with the more aggressive approach of 15-17 in this book. There's nothing wrong with a more conservative range of 16-18, and it helps to be familiar with both ranges.

Opening One-of-a-Suit

When you have a hand in the range of 13-21 points that doesn't meet the requirements for a 1NT opening, open the bidding at the one level in a suit. Opening bids of 1♣, 1♦, 1♥, and 1♠ cover a broad range of hand patterns. They can be made on balanced hands outside the range for 1NT or on wildly distributional hands.

The best trump suit tends to be the one with the most cards in the combined partnership hands. To help partner decide on the best fit, you usually start the bidding in the longest suit rather than the strongest. With a choice between two suits of equal length, open the higher-ranking. There are, however, a couple of exceptions.

Five-Card Majors

A popular bidding style in North America is to require that opener have at least five cards in a major suit to open 1♥ or 1♠. We'll use this *five-card major* approach throughout the book.

Minor Suit Openings

Hands of 13 or more points with no five-card major are opened in the longer minor suit. Occasionally, this requires opening 1♣ or 1♦ with a three-card suit. This is often referred to as the *better minor* or, less appropriately, the *short club*. One piece of advice: don't cloud your thinking with visions of the 'short' club. Simply open in the longer minor suit. With four cards in both minors, open 1♦; with three cards in both minors, open 1♣.

Examples

You are the dealer, or the player on your right has dealt and passed. You have to decide what call to make.

♠ A K 3
♥ K J 7
♦ K 9 8 5
♣ J 8 5

If the partnership has agreed to a range of 15-17 points for an opening bid of 1NT, this hand is ideal for 1NT. If your range is 16-18, you would start with an opening bid of 1♦.

♠ K 10
♥ Q J 8 6 3
♦ A Q 9
♣ K J 4

Open 1NT—even holding a five-card major suit. If you open 1♥ and partner responds 1♠, for example, you have an impossible task finding a rebid that shows the strength of your hand.

♠ K Q 9 5
♥ 8 4
♦ K J 10 8
♣ A Q J

Open 1NT. Today's players no longer worry about holding a worthless doubleton for a 1NT opening bid —or 2NT for that matter. 1NT doesn't end the auction; it merely sends a descriptive message to partner.

♠ A K Q 2
♥ 7 4
♦ J 9 8 7 5
♣ K 8

Open 1♦. As the bidding progresses, you'll have a chance to uncover a spade fit, if there is one.

♠ A 4
♥ J 9 8 6 3
♦ A K 9 8 4
♣ 4

Open 1♥, the higher-ranking of the two five-card suits. The guideline says nothing about the relative strength of the suits.

♠ A 10 8 4
♥ K J 10 3
♦ 7 6
♣ K Q 4

Open 1♣. With no five-card major suit, open the longer minor suit. On occasion, this will be a three-card suit. With three cards in both minors, open 1♣. With four-cards in both minors, open 1♦.

Improving Your Judgment

There's more to valuing a hand than adding the high card and length points. Here are some tips to help you make better choices when you have borderline decisions.

1. Togetherness of Honors

When honors are together in the same suit they have more trick-taking potential than when they are in separate suits. Compare these hands.

	1)		2)	
	♠	K 9 8 5 3	♠	A K Q 9 8
	♥	A Q	♥	5 3
	♦	Q 10 6	♦	K Q 10
	♣	K 7 2	♣	7 6 2

Both hands have 14 high-card points and 1 distribution point. This might suggest that they are equal in value. A closer look, focusing on where the high cards are located, tells a different story. On the first hand, the ♥A will take a trick. The other high cards may take tricks, depending on the position of the missing high cards. On the second hand, there are three or more spade tricks and at least one diamond trick. There's much more trick-taking potential when high cards are working together in the same suit than when they are isolated in different suits.

2. The Supporting Cast

High cards are the stars within each suit. The lower cards also have their role to play. Compare these two hands:

	1)		2)	
	♠	K 7 2	♠	K 10 8
	♥	A J 6	♥	A J 10
	♦	K Q 4	♦	K Q 10
	♣	Q J 5 2	♣	Q J 10 9

Both hands have 16 points, and the high cards are in the same suits. Only the low cards are different, but the second hand feels much stronger. Look at the club suit. In the first hand, you may not be able to develop club tricks if the missing high cards are unfavorably placed. In the second hand, you expect to promote two club tricks because the ♣10 and ♣9 accompany the ♣Q-J combination.

3. The Shape of Things

The pattern, or shape of a hand can be important. The more unbalanced the hand, the more challenging it is to evaluate. Long suits can improve the trick taking potential. Compare these two hands.

1)	♠ K Q J	2)	♠ K Q J 10 9
	♥ A 10 9		♥ A 4
	♦ 10 9 4 3		♦ 3
	♣ A Q J		♣ A Q J 10 9

The high cards are the same but the second hand is much better than the first. In the first hand you expect to take two spades, a heart and two or three clubs. In the second hand you expect to take four spades, one heart and four or five clubs.

4. The Rule of 20

When you are the first or second player to make a call in the auction, the strength of partner's hand is unlimited, since partner has not yet had a chance to speak. If you open, partner will expect a hand worth 13 or more points and bid accordingly. Holding 13 or more points, responder will push the partnership to at least the game level.

The following guideline can be used when you have a close decision:

RULE OF 20

In borderline cases in first or second position, add your high-card points to the number of cards in your two longest suits. If the total is 20 or more, consider opening the bidding; otherwise, pass.

---

1)	♠ A J 7 5 3	2)	♠ A J 7 5
	♥ K 4		♥ K 4 3
	♦ Q 10 7 3		♦ Q 10 7 3
	♣ J 5		♣ J 5

Following this guideline, you would open the first hand (11 + 5 + 4 = 20) but not the second (11 + 4 + 4 = 19).

Summary

Opening the Bidding at the One Level In First or Second Chair

Based on a style of five-card major suit opening bids, use the following guidelines for hands in the range of 13-21 points:

Bid 1NT with a balanced hand and 15-17 points

- even with a five-card major suit
- even with a worthless doubleton

With a five-card or longer suit, bid the longest suit

- bid the higher-ranking of two five-card or six-card suits

Otherwise, bid the longer minor suit

- bid 1♦ with two four-card suits or 1♣ with two three-card suits.

Note: 1. Semi-balanced hands (with more than one doubleton) can be opened 1NT if opening in a suit might lead to rebid problems.

2. With borderline opening bids you can be more aggressive if your high cards are working together, you have some intermediate cards, and you have long suits.

3. With borderline hands in first and second position, you can use the *Rule of 20* as a guideline. Add the high-card points to the number of cards in the two longest suits. If the total is 20 or more, open the bidding; otherwise, pass.

Quiz

1. You are the dealer. What call do you make with these hands?

a) ♠ J 4
   ♥ A J 3
   ♦ K J 7 6 2
   ♣ K Q 9

b) ♠ K Q 9 5 3
   ♥ 8
   ♦ A K 10 8 4
   ♣ K 6

c) ♠ J 7 5
   ♥ Q J 5 2
   ♦ K Q 7
   ♣ Q 9 5

d) ♠ A Q 8 7 3
   ♥ —
   ♦ 8 6
   ♣ A K 8 6 4 2

e) ♠ 10 8 7 5
   ♥ Q J 6 3
   ♦ A J 8
   ♣ A Q

f) ♠ 6
   ♥ A K 8 6
   ♦ 9 7 4
   ♣ K J 8 5 2

g) ♠ K J
   ♥ A 9 2
   ♦ A J 8 6
   ♣ K Q J 5

h) ♠ Q 10 7 5 3
   ♥ A 8 4 2
   ♦ K 7
   ♣ J 9

i) ♠ K J 10
   ♥ Q J 9
   ♦ A J 10 8 3
   ♣ Q 6

j) ♠ K 10 3
   ♥ K J 6
   ♦ A Q 10 8 4
   ♣ A 5

k) ♠ Q J 7 5
   ♥ A J 8
   ♦ A 9 2
   ♣ J 10 5

l) ♠ A J 9 7 5
   ♥ Q 2
   ♦ K J 8 4
   ♣ 7 2

2. The dealer on your right passes. What call do you make?

a) ♠ K Q 9 5
   ♥ A J 10 7
   ♦ 4 3
   ♣ A Q 5

b) ♠ A Q
   ♥ K Q 5
   ♦ J 7 6 5 4 2
   ♣ K 9

c) ♠ A K 6 5
   ♥ A 4
   ♦ 9 7 6 3 2
   ♣ J 6

d) ♠ A 8 6
   ♥ K Q 9 3
   ♦ J 9
   ♣ Q 10 7 5

e) ♠ A 8 6
   ♥ K Q 9 3
   ♦ J 9 5
   ♣ Q 10 7

f) ♠ 4
   ♥ K J 9 8 7 3
   ♦ A J 10 5 4
   ♣ 8

g) ♠ K Q
   ♥ A Q
   ♦ J 8 6 3
   ♣ K 10 8 7 5

h) ♠ K Q 9 5
   ♥ K J 7 3
   ♦ 8 6 3
   ♣ A J

i) ♠ Q J 2
   ♥ K 9 7 3
   ♦ Q J 5
   ♣ Q J 4

j) ♠ K 7 5 3 2
   ♥ K
   ♦ A 9 7 6 2
   ♣ 8 3

k) ♠ A Q 8 5
   ♥ A K Q 5
   ♦ 4
   ♣ K Q J 7

l) ♠ 4
   ♥ A 8 3
   ♦ A K Q 10
   ♣ 7 5 4 3 2

Answers to Quiz

1a) 1NT. This is a balanced hand with 15 high-card points plus 1 length point for the five-card suit.

1b) 1♠. Open the higher-ranking of two five-card suits.

1c) Pass. This hand doesn't qualify as an opening bid in first or second position under the *Rule of 20* (11 + 4 + 3 = 18).

1d) 1♣. Open the longest suit first, even with a five-card major.

1e) 1♦. Open the longer minor suit with a hand too weak for 1NT.

1f) 1♣. Qualifies as an opening bid under the *Rule of 20* (11 + 5 + 4 = 20).

1g) 1♦. Too strong for 1NT. Open 1♦ with four cards in both minors.

1h) Pass. Doesn't qualify under the *Rule of 20* (10 + 5 + 4 = 19).

1i) 1NT. 14 high-card points plus 1 for length qualifies for 1NT if your range is 15-17.

1j) 1♦. 17 high-card points plus 1 length point is too much for 1NT.

1k) 1♣. With no five-card major, open 1♣ with three cards in each minor.

1l) 1♠. Qualifies as an opener using the *Rule of 20* (11 + 5 + 4 = 20).

2a) 1NT. Don't worry about the low doubleton in diamonds.

2b) 1NT. Treat the hand as balanced. If you open 1♦, you will have a difficult time showing the strength of your hand.

2c) 1♦. Longest suit first—even if it's not the strongest suit.

2d) 1♣. The *Rule of 20* indicates this is an opening bid (12 + 4 + 4 = 20).

2e) Pass. Move one card from the previous hand and it no longer qualifies as an opening bid using the *Rule of 20* (12 + 4 + 3 = 19).

2f) 1♥. Only 9 high-card points but the *Rule of 20* is satisfied (9 + 6 + 5 = 20).

2g) 1NT. Treat the hand as balanced or you'll have an awkward rebid.

2h) 1♦. An unpleasant choice of opening bid, but the five-card major style has some disadvantages.

2i) Pass. You don't have enough to open even using the *Rule of 20*.

2j) Pass (1♠). Although the hand qualifies using the Rule of 20, the honors are not together and there are no 10's or 9's.

2k) 1♣. 21 points, but still a one level opening bid.

2l) 1♦ (1♣). Treat the diamonds as a five-card suit. The rebid could be awkward if you open 1♣ and partner responds 1♠.

HAND: 1-1   NORTH
DEALER: NORTH   ♠ K 9 7 5 2
VUL: NONE   ♥ Q 6
                      ♦ K Q 9 6 4
                      ♣ 10

WEST   EAST
♠ J   ♠ Q 10 3
♥ K 7 5 2   ♥ J 10 9 3
♦ 10 5 3   ♦ A 7 2
♣ A Q 7 5 4   ♣ K 8 6

                      SOUTH
                      ♠ A 8 6 4
                      ♥ A 8 4
                      ♦ J 8
                      ♣ J 9 3 2

WEST	NORTH	EAST	SOUTH
	1♠ (?)	Pass	2♠/3♠
Pass	Pass	Pass	

Bidding

The North hand has only 10 high-card and 2 length points. If North passes, the hand will likely be passed out, since none of the other players has a full opening bid. With a borderline hand, North might apply the *Rule of 20*. With two five-card suits and 10 high-card points, the guideline suggests that the hand is worth an opening bid (10 + 5 + 5 = 20).

If North opens 1♠, South also has a judgment call to make. With 10 high-card points plus a doubleton diamond, the hand is on the borderline between a conservative raise to 2♠ and a more aggressive limit raise to 3♠. Whichever call South chooses, North should pass, having opened such a minimum hand.

Opening Lead

East has to make the opening lead and will likely choose the ♥J, top of the *solid sequence* in that suit.

Play

There's not much to the play on this hand. If declarer, plays a low heart from dummy on the opening lead, West will win the ♥K and probably play the ♣A. Declarer still has to lose a trump trick—when the missing spades divide 3-1—and the ♦A. The missing diamonds divide 3-3, so declarer doesn't need to ruff any diamond losers in the dummy.

Defense

If East leads the ♥J and declarer plays a low heart from dummy, West wins the first trick with the ♥K. From the lead of the ♥J, West can infer that declarer holds the ♥Q, so there's not much future in hearts. West should probably switch to the ♣A, hoping to take any of the defenders tricks in that suit before declarer can discard losers. East should play an encouraging (high) club, but the defenders can't get any more club tricks. The best they can do is get their ♦A and a trump trick to restrict declarer to nine tricks.

If West returns a heart at trick two, declarer will be able to discard a club loser on the ♥A and make ten tricks. If West doesn't lead a heart initially, declarer may also make ten tricks by using the diamond suit to discard two hearts from dummy. So, if North-South happen to reach game, East-West have to defend well to defeat the contract.

HAND: 1-2
DEALER: EAST
VUL: N-S

NORTH
- ♠ J 6
- ♥ Q 9 3
- ♦ A 9 4 2
- ♣ K 7 4 3

WEST
- ♠ 10 2
- ♥ J 7 4
- ♦ Q 8 6 5 3
- ♣ J 9 2

EAST
- ♠ A K 7 3
- ♥ A K 5 2
- ♦ K 7
- ♣ Q 10 5

SOUTH
- ♠ Q 9 8 5 4
- ♥ 10 8 6
- ♦ J 10
- ♣ A 8 6

WEST	NORTH	EAST	SOUTH
		1♣	Pass
Pass	Pass (?)		

Bidding

East has a balanced hand with 19 high-card points—too strong to open 1NT but not strong enough for 2NT. With no five-card major, East opens the longer minor suit, 1♣. South's hand isn't good enough for an overcall, especially vulnerable, so the auction comes to West.

With only 4 high-card points plus 1 length point for the five-card suit, West doesn't have enough to respond. The 1♣ bid isn't forcing, so West should pass. Bidding is likely to get the partnership into trouble. If East has a minimum opening bid, the partnership may already be too high. If East has a strong bid, East's rebid will likely get the partnership overboard. On the actual hand, if West were to respond 1♦, East would jump to 2NT, taking the partnership beyond a safe level.

When the 1♣ bid is passed around to North, North should probably leave well enough alone and choose to defend 1♣. North could *balance* 1NT, since South is marked with some strength when

East–West stop at the one level. It is likely, however, that South also holds some length in clubs. With shortness in clubs and the strength for an opening bid, South would have made a takeout double. Defending 1♣ looks to be the best choice.

Opening Lead

South has no clear-cut opening lead and will probably start with the ♠5, fourth highest, hoping to develop some tricks in that suit.

Play

Low level partscore contracts are difficult to play, especially on a three-three trump fit! In this situation, it isn't usually a good idea to draw trump. Instead, declarer should try to scramble home with seven tricks.

Unless the suits are breaking very badly—unlikely when the opponents have not entered the bidding—East can probably count on the ♠A-K and ♥A-K as four tricks. One trick can be promoted in the diamond suit, and there's one sure trick in the club suit, even though the defenders hold the ♣A and ♣K. Declarer needs to find one more trick. If South leads a spade, declarer can take two tricks with the ♠A and ♠K and lead another spade, trumping in the dummy. Declarer must be careful to trump with a high club, not the ♣2, to avoid having North overruff with a low club.

Provided declarer ruffs the third round of spades with the ♣9 or ♣J, the contract can now be made. If North doesn't overruff with the ♣K, East gets two spades, two hearts, one diamond, the spade ruff, and an eventual second trick in the club suit. If North does overruff with the ♣K, declarer can now promote two club winners by driving out South's ♣A.

Defense

The only lead that gives the defenders a chance to defeat the contract is a club. This isn't easy for South to find. Even after a club lead, the defenders may have difficulty getting all their tricks—it becomes an interesting race.

HAND: 1-3
DEALER: SOUTH
VUL: E-W

NORTH
♠ Q J 4
♥ 10 8 5 3
♦ A 6 4
♣ 6 5 3

WEST
♠ A 9 6 2
♥ K 9 4
♦ 8 7 2
♣ A 9 7

EAST
♠ 10 5 3
♥ J 7 6 2
♦ J 3
♣ K 10 8 4

SOUTH
♠ K 8 7
♥ A Q
♦ K Q 10 9 5
♣ Q J 2

WEST	NORTH	EAST	SOUTH
			1♦
Pass	1♥	Pass	2NT
Pass	3NT	Pass	Pass
Pass			

Bidding

With a balanced hand of 17 high-card points plus 1 point for the five-card diamond suit, South is too strong to open 1NT if the partnership range is 15-17. Instead, South starts with 1♦.

West doesn't really have the right type of hand for a takeout double, so the bidding comes to North who responds 1♥, showing the four-card major suit. South now finishes the description of the hand by jumping to 2NT, showing a balanced hand of 18-19 points. This isn't a forcing bid but, with 7 high-card points, North may accept the invitation and bid game. Even if the partnership has only 25 combined points, game should be a reasonable gamble.

If South were to open 1NT instead of 1♦, the auction might well end there. So, North and South's judgment will determine whether the hand is played in partscore or game.

Opening Lead

With no particular guidance from the auction, West will lead the ♠2, fourth highest from longest and strongest.

Play

Declarer starts with only four sure tricks, the ♥A and ♦A-K-Q. Provided the missing diamonds divide 3-2 or the ♦J is singleton, declarer should get two more tricks from that suit. The defenders have attacked spades, but declarer can get two tricks in the suit through promotion. One more trick is needed.

The heart finesse offers a 50% chance for a ninth trick—if East holds the ♥K. The club suit, however, actually offers a 75% chance for the ninth trick. If East holds the ♣A or the ♣K or both, a trick can be developed by leading twice toward the ♣Q-J-2. Only if West holds both the ♣A and ♣K will this plan fail. There is a danger that the defenders may be able to establish enough winners in spades to defeat the contract while declarer is developing a club trick, but this is very unlikely. West's lead of the ♠2, fourth highest, indicates that West holds only a four-card suit.

Declarer plays the ♠J on the first trick, hoping to win the trick in dummy. When the ♠J wins, declarer can lead a low club from dummy. If East plays low, South plays the ♣J, driving out West's ♣A. Assuming West continues leading spades, declarer can win a trick in dummy and lead another club toward the ♣Q. If East plays low, the ♣Q will immediately be the ninth trick. If East wins the ♣K, the ♣Q will be the ninth trick when declarer regains the lead.

Defense

If declarer finds the correct line of play, the defenders cannot defeat the contract unless East makes the brilliant—and unlikely—play of hopping up with the ♣K on the first round of the suit and leading a heart. If East does find this play, North-South can offer their congratulations . . . and then find an easier pair of opponents!

HAND: 1-4
DEALER: WEST
VUL: BOTH

NORTH
♠ Q 9 8 4
♥ 8 4 3
♦ A 8
♣ Q J 10 3

WEST
♠ A K 10 5 2
♥ 10
♦ K Q 10 6 4 3
♣ 4

EAST
♠ 7 3
♥ A 7 6 5 2
♦ J 9
♣ K 8 7 6

SOUTH
♠ J 6
♥ K Q J 9
♦ 7 5 2
♣ A 9 5 2

WEST	NORTH	EAST	SOUTH
1♦	Pass	1♥	Pass
1♠	Pass	1NT	Pass
2♠	Pass	3♦	Pass
Pass	Pass		

Bidding

To describe 6-5 distribution, the standard approach is to open the six-card suit, planning to bid and rebid the five-card suit. So, West starts with 1♦. East responds 1♥. West introduces the second suit by bidding 1♠. At this point, East is unaware that West has a very distributional hand. West might bid the same way with four diamonds and four spades. With no fit with either suit, East will probably choose to bid 1NT rather than rebidding the weak five-card heart suit.

Now West finishes the description by rebidding 2♠. By bidding spades twice, West is showing a five-card suit. By inference, West must also hold at least six diamonds. With five spades and five diamonds, West would start with the higher-ranking suit, 1♠. Opposite such an unbalanced hand, a notrump contract is unlikely to fare well. East should give *preference* back to 3♦, putting the partnership in its eight-card fit. Passing 2♠ would leave the partnership one level lower but in a seven-card trump fit—which could be disastrous if the trump suit breaks badly.

Having fully described the hand and receiving no encouragement from partner, West settles for partscore.

Opening Lead

The auction has given North a lot of information. To prevent declarer from ruffing spade losers in dummy, West should probably lead a trump. The alternative is to lead the ♣Q, hoping to establish tricks in that suit. It's possible that declarer might run out of trumps if forced to ruff the defenders' club winners at every opportunity.

Play

If the defenders lead trump, the ♦A and another diamond, declarer can draw the remaining trump and then try to establish a winner through length in the spade suit. Since the missing spades divide 4-2, declarer's fifth spade will eventually be established as a winner. Declarer loses two spade tricks, one diamond trick, and one club trick.

If the defenders don't lead diamonds right away, declarer will have an opportunity to ruff one or more spade losers in dummy and will likely finish with at least one overtrick.

Defense

The best lead for the defense is the ♦A and another diamond. If North leads the ♣Q, the defenders will still have an opportunity to lead trump after winning the first trick. If they don't lead diamonds, declarer will likely make more than nine tricks.

If West plays in a spade contract, North should lead the ♣Q, hoping to force declarer to ruff. Since North holds four spades, the defenders will have as many trumps as declarer once West has ruffed once. This will make the play very uncomfortable for declarer and the defense should defeat even a 2♠ contract by at least one trick.

Past Times

About Third Hand

> "A hand should be opened in third position with a King less than the normal requirements, provided you have a fairly good suit."
>
> —Charles Goren, IN A NUTSHELL, 1946

About Fourth Hand

> "It may be considered rather cautious bidding by some persons, but when in doubt there is nothing better than a new deal."
>
> —R.F. Foster, FOSTER'S AUCTION MADE EASY, 1920

Chapter Two

Opening at the One Level — In Third and Fourth Position

The first step in valuing a hand is to look at the high-card points and distribution, but the process doesn't stop there. Your judgment . . . and results . . . will improve when you take other factors into account. The location of the high cards can make a difference; a king and queen working together in the same suit are often more valuable than a king in one suit and a queen in another. The lower-ranking cards can affect the value; 9's and 10's usually carry more weight than 2's and 3's. And then there's your position at the table.

If you are the dealer, in *first position* or *first chair*, partner has not yet spoken. If the dealer on your right passes and you are in *second position*, or *second chair*, the strength of partner's hand is also unknown. Bidding is a conversation, not a single statement, and you have certain obligations if you open the bidding in first or second position. Partner will expect a certain minimum amount of strength—typically 13 or more points—and will bid accordingly. If partner responds in a new suit, you are expected to bid again and must be prepared to do so. As a result, it's best to have sound values to open the bidding at the one level in first or second chair.

The situation changes once partner has passed and you have a chance to open the bidding in third or fourth chair. Now you already know something about partner's hand; partner doesn't have enough for an opening bid. This changes the complexion of the bidding conversation. One important point to keep in mind is:

OPENING OPPOSITE A PASSED HAND

A new suit by responder is no longer forcing.

Let's see how this affects opener's thinking in third and fourth position with borderline hands.

Borderline Openings in Third Position

If both partner and the player on your right pass, you have an opportunity to open in third position. If you pass, the auction isn't over; the opponent on your left can still open. Since a new suit by responder is no longer forcing, you don't have to be as concerned about making a rebid and this affects your strategy with a marginal hand. It's standard practice to occasionally open *light,* with less than the values for a first or second chair opening bid. There are several advantages to this tactic.

Making a Partscore

When partner has passed, the chance of making game is remote when you don't have a full opening bid. If neither partner ever opens with 11 or 12 points, however, your side will miss a lot of opportunities to make a partscore and these little hands can add up over the long run.

Helping Partner on Defense

If the opponents get to play the contract, your opening bid may help with the defense. It may get partner off to the best opening lead and help partner place the missing cards.

Confusing the Opponents

If the hand belongs to the opponents, your opening bid may get in their way, causing them to misjudge and bid too much or two little.

Example

♠ A Q J 10 6 You would probably choose to pass in first or second
♥ 7 2   position since the hand doesn't even qualify as an
♦ Q J 4   opening bid using the *Rule of 20* (10 + 5 + 3 = 18).
♣ 7 4 3   In third chair, however, it may be worthwhile to open

1♠. You may make a partscore; you'll get partner off to the best lead if the opponents buy the contract; you may make it difficult for the opponents to find their best spot. If partner raises or bids 1NT, you can pass. If partner bids 2♣ or 2♦, you can pass and play for partscore. If partner bids 2♥ . . . pass and hope for the best.

Borderline Openings in Fourth Position

Fourth position adds a new element to the equation. You have the same tactical considerations for opening light as in third position with the additional option of passing the hand out. If you pass, it's a 'tie' and neither side scores any points. If you choose to open the bidding, you want to be confident that your side will get a plus score . . . for making a contract or for defeating the opponents if they win the auction.

There are 40 high-card points in the deck. If you have a border-line hand in fourth position, it's likely the missing points are fairly evenly divided among the other three players since none of them opened the bidding. Both sides will have a chance for a partscore and, when it comes to auctions in which both sides are likely to compete, *the spade suit is critical.* If both sides have a trump fit, the side that has a fit in spades has the advantage. To compete in any other suit, you have to go up a level, committing to take one more trick.

The Rule of 15

In fourth position, some players like to use a guideline developed by Don Pearson of Berkeley, California, commonly referred to as *Pearson Points* or the *Rule of 15*:

> ### RULE OF 15
> In borderline cases in fourth position, add your high-card points to the number of spades you hold. If the total is 15 or more, open the bidding; otherwise, consider passing.

1) ♠ Q 8 5 2   2) ♠ 6
♥ K 8 4   ♥ K 8 4
♦ 6   ♦ Q 8 5 2
♣ A Q 7 3 2   ♣ A Q 7 3 2

After three passes, the *Rule of 15* suggests opening the first hand (11 + 4 = 15) but passing the second (11 + 1 = 12), even though they are identical except for interchanging the spades and diamonds.

Examples

What call would you make with these hands in third chair after two passes. What would you call in fourth chair after three passes?

♠ K J 10 8 4
♥ J 7 3
♦ Q 7 5
♣ K J

Open 1♠ in third or fourth position. This wouldn't be a sound opening in first or second, but you can open light in third chair. It also satisfies the *Rule of 15* in fourth chair (11 + 5 = 16). You can pass any response from partner, hoping for a small plus score.

♠ 8 3
♥ 7 5 2
♦ K 5 3
♣ A K J 9 4

Open 1♣ in third chair. You'd certainly prefer a club lead from partner if the opponents buy the contract. In fourth, the *Rule of 15* suggests passing the hand out. Don't give the opponents a second chance.

♠ Q 5
♥ K Q 9
♦ J 9 7 5 3
♣ A K 5

Open 1NT in third or fourth chair. Light openings and the *Rule of 15* only apply to borderline opening bids. The requirements for opening 1NT don't change in third or fourth position.

♠ K 9 7 4
♥ K J 6 3
♦ 5
♣ A 10 8 4

Open 1♣ in third or fourth chair. The hand is borderline but, holding support for both major suits, it's probably worth opening light in third. In fourth, the hand just meets the requirements (11 + 4 = 15).

♠ K 9 5
♥ Q 10 6
♦ J 9 4 3
♣ A 8 2

Pass in any position. There's no need to get carried away with opening light when you have a poor hand. You don't even want to suggest an opening lead to partner.

♠ 8
♥ Q 3 2
♦ K Q 9 7 5
♣ A J 5 4

You would open this hand 1♦ in first, second, or third chair. In fourth, however, it's probably best to pass the hand out. The hand fails the *Rule of 15* (12 + 1 = 13), so get on with the next deal.

Improving Your Judgment

You can improve your results by considering your position at the table before choosing an opening call. Here are some tips.

1. Eye on the Goal

It's easy to fall into the trap of simply counting to 13 and then opening the bidding. A better approach is to keep your objective in mind. Compare these two hands.

1)	♠ A Q 10 7 6		2)	♠ 8 4
	♥ J 9 3			♥ J 9 3
	♦ K 7 5			♦ K 7 5
	♣ 8 4			♣ A Q 10 7 6

In first or second position, you shouldn't open either hand since your objective is to make a descriptive call that will serve as the basis for a constructive auction. Partner will expect a full opening bid. In third chair you might open either hand with the hope of getting a small partscore or helping partner on opening lead. In fourth chair, you want to get a plus score . . . or at least not go minus. That would be a reason for opening the first hand but passing with the second hand (10 +2 = 12).

2. Be Prepared

The good news is that a new suit by responder is not forcing once partner passed originally. You should be prepared, however, for a response from partner. Consider these two hands:

1)	♠ A J 10 7 5		2)	♠ A J 10 7 5
	♥ Q 4			♥ 4
	♦ K 7 5			♦ K 7 5
	♣ J 8 3			♣ Q 8 3 2

Both are borderline openings in both third and fourth position. To avoid getting too high with the first hand after opening 1♠, you are prepared to pass any response by partner. Even if partner responds 2♥ you can pass since partner should have a five-card suit. On the second hand, however, you'll be awkwardly placed if you open 1♠ and partner responds 2♥. That might sway your judgment to pass rather than open.

3. Bending the Rules

When opening in first or second chair, there are guidelines when you have a choice of suits to bid. In third and fourth chair, you may occasionally consider bending the 'rules.' Look at these two hands.

1)	♠ Q 8 3		2)	♠ Q 8 3
	♥ J 7 5 3			♥ A K Q 10
	♦ 9 4			♦ 9 4
	♣ A K Q 10			♣ J 7 5 3

Both are borderline hands that are probably worth opening in third or fourth chair. With the first hand, you'd make the standard opening bid of 1♣. With the second hand, you might want to consider the advantage of opening 1♥ rather than 1♣. Even though the partnership style is five-card majors, there's always some room for judgment.

4. Strength Before Length

The general guideline for opening the bidding is *length before strength*. The partnership is looking for the longest combined trump suit, not the strongest. Of course, you've already seen exceptions due to the constraints of playing five-card majors—sometimes having to open a three-card minor suit. In third and fourth position, there's reason to consider additional exceptions. Compare these two hands.

1)	♠ 7		2)	♠ 7
	♥ K J 4			♥ K J 4
	♦ A Q J 10 3			♦ A Q J 10
	♣ 9 8 6 4			♣ 9 8 6 4 3

In third position, you could think about opening the bidding with both of these hands. On the first hand, there's no difficulty following the general guidelines and opening 1♦. With the second hand, the guideline of opening the longest suit would mean an opening bid of 1♣. That's not the suit you would like partner to lead on defense. You will also be awkwardly placed if partner responds 1♠. You don't want to rebid 1NT with an unbalanced hand and, if you bid 2♦, you may push the partnership too high. Time to exercise your judgment and open 1♦ with this hand also.

Summary

Opening the Bidding
In Third or Fourth Position

In third position:

It is a good tactic to occasionally open *light*, with as few as 10 or 11 points, hoping to make a partscore, find the best defense, or cause the opponents to misjudge the situation. Since partner passed originally, *a new suit response is no longer forcing.*

In fourth position:

With borderline hands, use the *Rule of 15*. Add the high-card points to the number of spades. If the total is 15 or more, consider opening the bidding; otherwise, pass.

Quiz

1. Partner and the player on your right both pass. What call do you make on the following hands in third chair?

a) ♠ K 9 8 6 3
   ♥ A Q J 9 5
   ♦ A
   ♣ 6 4

b) ♠ Q 7 6 4
   ♥ A K 10 9 3
   ♦ J 3
   ♣ 3 2

c) ♠ K Q 5
   ♥ Q 9 6 4
   ♦ K 9 7
   ♣ J 8 3

d) ♠ 9 7 3
   ♥ J 4
   ♦ A K J 10
   ♣ Q 7 3 2

e) ♠ 6 3
   ♥ K Q J 10
   ♦ 8 7 5 4 2
   ♣ A 3

f) ♠ Q J 7
   ♥ K Q J 10 5
   ♦ K 4
   ♣ A 10 9

g) ♠ Q 7
   ♥ Q 9 5
   ♦ K Q 7 2
   ♣ A J 8 3

h) ♠ J 9 7 5 2
   ♥ K J 3
   ♦ Q 9 5
   ♣ Q 7

i) ♠ 6 2
   ♥ A K 8 7
   ♦ K 3
   ♣ A K J 8 5

j) ♠ 7 3
   ♥ K 8 2
   ♦ 9 5
   ♣ A Q J 9 7 3

k) ♠ K 10 7 5
   ♥ Q J 9 8
   ♦ 8 3
   ♣ A J 5

l) ♠ A J 7 2
   ♥ K J 10 8 5
   ♦ 5
   ♣ 10 5 3

2. The dealer on your left passes and this is followed by two more passes. It's up to you in fourth position. What call do you make?

a) ♠ A J 9 8
   ♥ 7
   ♦ A K 8 6 3
   ♣ K Q 6

b) ♠ J 8 5
   ♥ Q 9 7 6 3
   ♦ K 6 2
   ♣ Q 7

c) ♠ Q 10 7 5
   ♥ K 8
   ♦ Q 9 4
   ♣ A J 7 2

d) ♠ J 8
   ♥ K 9 7 6 5
   ♦ K J 8 4
   ♣ K 6

e) ♠ Q 10 4
   ♥ K 6
   ♦ A Q J 8 7
   ♣ K 9 2

f) ♠ 9 8 6 4 2
   ♥ K Q 7 4
   ♦ A J
   ♣ 9 8

g) ♠ A J
   ♥ K J 9 7 3
   ♦ K Q 5
   ♣ K 10 6

h) ♠ 3
   ♥ A J 8 3
   ♦ K J 10 2
   ♣ Q J 6 2

i) ♠ 7 5 4 2
   ♥ Q 9 7
   ♦ A 8 3
   ♣ K Q 5

j) ♠ 10 8 5
   ♥ A K Q 9
   ♦ K 8 3
   ♣ 7 5 4

k) ♠ —
   ♥ A K 9 5
   ♦ A Q 8 7 2
   ♣ Q 8 5 4

l) ♠ 9
   ♥ 3
   ♦ K Q 9 8 7 5
   ♣ A Q 8 7 3

Answers to Quiz

1a) 1♠. A standard opening bid—the higher-ranking of two five-card suits.

1b) 1♥. Only 10 high-card points, but worth a gamble in third chair.

1c) Pass. With no attractive bid, there's no reason to open light.

1d) 1♦. Get that lead-directing bid in . . . and hope for the best.

1e) 1♥ (Pass). If you're going to open light, those honors in the heart suit make it look like a five-card suit.

1f) 1NT. Keep an eye out for those balanced hands in the 15-17 range.

1g) 1♦. The standard opening bid. Don't open 1NT light in third or fourth chair.

1h) Pass. No reason to emphasize that feeble spade suit.

1i) 1♣. With a good hand, make the standard opening bid.

1j) 1♣ (3♣). Show those clubs. Some players might choose to open with a preemptive 3♣ in third chair.

1k) 1♣. With good support for both majors, it's probably worthwhile opening this hand.

1l) 1♥ (Pass). You might risk opening this hand, but if partner responds 2♦ you will have an awkward rebid.

2a) 1♦. No need to hesitate on this hand. Make the standard opening bid in your longest suit.

2b) Pass. No need to think about this hand either. On to the next hand.

2c) 1♣. A borderline opening, but it satisfies the *Rule of 15* (12 + 4 = 16).

2d) Pass. A borderline hand that doesn't meet the *Rule of 15* (11 + 2 = 13).

2e) 1NT. Notrump opening bids are the same in all positions.

2f) 1♠. Only 10 high-card points, but it meets the *Rule of 15* (10 + 5 = 15).

2g) 1♥. Too strong for 1NT—17 high-card points plus 1 for the five-card heart suit.

2h) Pass. Too few spades to satisfy the *Rule of 15* (12 + 1 = 13).

2i) 1♣. The spades aren't great, but the *Rule of 15* is satisfied (11 + 4 = 15).

2j) 1♥. If you're going to open this hand in fourth, treat the hearts as a five-card suit.

2k) 1♦. The spade void shouldn't deter you from opening a good hand.

2l) Pass (3♦). The *Rule of 15* says not to open this hand, even though you'd open in any other position. If you can't resist, a preemptive opening of 3♦ might be better than 1♦.

HAND:	2-1	NORTH
DEALER:	NORTH	♠ J 7
VUL:	NONE	♥ A K Q 9 4
		♦ 10 6 3
		♣ 9 4 2

WEST		EAST
♠ Q 10 9		♠ K 4 2
♥ J 3 2		♥ 8 7
♦ A Q J 8		♦ 9 5 4 2
♣ 10 6 3		♣ K Q J 7

SOUTH
♠ A 8 6 5 3
♥ 10 6 5
♦ K 7
♣ A 8 5

WEST	NORTH	EAST	SOUTH
	Pass	Pass	1♠ (?)
Pass	2♥	Pass	Pass
Pass			

Bidding

This hand could easily get passed out since no one at the table has a sound opening hand with 13 or more points. South's hand doesn't qualify as an opening bid in first or second position using the *Rule of 20* (11 + 5 + 3 = 19). After two passes, however, South might choose to open *light* in third position. The tactical advantage of this bid is that the partnership might be able to make a small partscore, or the bid might get North off to the best opening lead on defense, or the opponents may misjudge the auction . . . bidding too much or too little.

If South does open 1♠, North will make the normal response of 2♥ . . . under the assumption that South has a full opening bid. South, however, can now pass, settling for partscore. Since North passed originally, a new suit response is no longer forcing. If South were to bid again at this point, North would assume South had a full opening and might get the partnership too high.

Opening Lead

East is on lead against the 2♥ contract and will start with the ♣K, top of the *solid three-card sequence.*

Play

Assuming the missing hearts are divided 3-2, North still has a spade loser, three diamond losers, and two club losers . . . one too many. North could plan to lead toward the ♦K, hoping East has the ♦A, a 50% chance. An alternative plan is to ruff one of the diamond losers in the dummy after giving up two tricks in the suit.

North can't afford to combine both chances in the diamond suit. After winning the ♣A, declarer would have to use a trump to get to the North hand to try the diamond finesse. If that loses, the defenders may lead another round of trumps. Declarer can give up another diamond trick, but the defenders may be able to lead a third round of trumps, preventing declarer from ruffing the loser in dummy.

To be sure of getting to ruff a diamond loser in dummy, declarer must lead a diamond *right away* after winning the ♣A. It seems unusual to lead a diamond *away from* the ♦K, but that is what declarer should do at trick two. If the defenders lead a trump, North wins and gives up a second diamond trick. The defenders can lead a second round of hearts, but North wins and still has a heart left in dummy to ruff the diamond loser. Declarer loses a spade, two diamonds, and two clubs, but makes the contract.

Defense

It's unlikely that East will find the only opening lead to defeat the contract . . . a trump. It's quite possible, however, that the defenders will get a second chance if declarer crosses to the North hand with a high heart to try the diamond finesse. Now West must foresee the likelihood of a diamond ruff in dummy and should lead trump at every opportunity. There's no hurry to take the club winners. The defenders can win the race if declarer doesn't lead diamonds right away.

HAND: 2-2
DEALER: EAST
VUL: N-S

NORTH
- ♠ K J 7
- ♥ A 8 6
- ♦ K Q 8 5
- ♣ A 6 2

WEST
- ♠ A 5 2
- ♥ K Q J 9 3
- ♦ 10 6
- ♣ 9 7 5

EAST
- ♠ 10 9 8 4
- ♥ 7 5
- ♦ 9 7 2
- ♣ K 10 4 3

SOUTH
- ♠ Q 6 3
- ♥ 10 4 2
- ♦ A J 4 3
- ♣ Q J 8

WEST	NORTH	EAST	SOUTH
		Pass	Pass
1 ♥ (?)	1NT	Pass	3NT
Pass	Pass	Pass	

Bidding

The West hand doesn't qualify as an opening bid in first or second position, even using the *Rule of 20* (10 + 5 + 3 = 18). With such a nice heart suit, however, West might choose to open *light* in third position for tactical reasons. East-West might get to buy the contract cheaply or might push North-South overboard.

On this hand, West's opening bid won't prevent North from overcalling 1NT, the same bid North would make if West passed. East has nothing to say, but South has enough to put the partnership in game in notrump, ending the auction.

Opening Lead

If West had not opened the bidding, East would lead the ♣3, fourth highest from the strongest suit, or the ♠10, top of a sequence. West's 1 ♥ opening gives East some useful information. East should now lead the ♥7, top of the doubleton in partner's suit.

Play

If East leads a heart, declarer is in trouble. Declarer has only six top tricks. A successful club finesse would provide only one extra trick, so declarer will eventually have to lead spades to try to promote two tricks in that suit. When declarer leads a spade, West can win the ♠A and take four established heart winners to defeat the contract.

It's a different story if East leads a club. Declarer can win the first trick with dummy's ♣J or ♣Q and immediately lead spades to promote two winners in that suit. It's too late for West to lead hearts. After the ♠A is driven out, declarer has two spade winners, the ♥A, four diamond tricks, and two club tricks.

If East leads a spade, declarer can still make the contract with careful play. Suppose West wins the ♠A and switches to a heart. North should hold up with the ♥A for two rounds, winning on the third round of the suit as East shows out. Now declarer can cross to dummy with a diamond winner to lead the ♣Q, taking the finesse. It doesn't matter that the finesse loses to East's ♣K, East has no hearts left to lead. Declarer again has two spades, one heart, four diamonds, and two club winners.

Defense

The only lead that allows the defenders to defeat the contract is a heart. Unless West opens the bidding 1♥ in third chair, it's very unlikely that East will find the winning lead. With no clear-cut alternative, East should be sure to lead partner's suit if West does open 1♥. Otherwise, West's light opening will have gone to waste.

HAND: 2-3
DEALER: SOUTH
VUL: E-W

NORTH
♠ K 7 4 2
♥ Q 10 7 5
♦ 10 4 2
♣ K 5

WEST
♠ 9 8
♥ A J 9
♦ K J 5
♣ Q 10 9 7 2

EAST
♠ Q 3
♥ K 6 4 2
♦ A Q 8 7 3
♣ J 4

SOUTH
♠ A J 10 6 5
♥ 8 3
♦ 9 6
♣ A 8 6 3

WEST	NORTH	EAST	SOUTH
			Pass
Pass	Pass	Pass (?)	

Bidding

South doesn't have enough to open the bidding and West doesn't have a sound opening bid in second position. West's hand doesn't quite qualify under the *Rule of 20* guideline (11 + 5 + 3 = 19). North doesn't have enough even for a light opening bid in third position, so the auction should be passed all the way round to East.

East has a hand that would be opened in first, second, or third position . . . 12 high-card points plus 1 for the five-card suit. In fourth position, however, East should only open the bidding on borderline hands if there is a good chance of getting a plus score, either by making a contract or defeating the opponents if they compete. Otherwise, East is better off to pass the hand out.

The spade suit plays a critical role in close decisions and East's hand doesn't qualify for an opening bid using the *Rule of 15* (12 high-card points + 2 spades = 14). The guideline suggests passing the hand out and moving on to the next deal.

If East does open 1♦, South is likely to overcall 1♠ . . . and the competition is on. West may respond 2♣ but North will raise to 2♠. If East-West compete further, they may get too high. Even if they do, North-South are likely to compete to a 3♠ contract, which they can make. It's too late for East to go back and pass the hand out.

The auction may not go that badly for East-West. North-South might not compete or might get too high, letting East-West get a plus score. This deal illustrates, however, the potential danger of opening a 'can of worms' in fourth chair when you have a borderline hand.

Opening Lead

If East opens the bidding and South wins the contract in a spade partscore, West will be on lead. West might lead the ♣10, top of the *interior sequence*, or a diamond, partner's suit.

Play

In a spade contract, South has a potential spade loser, two heart losers, two diamond losers, and two club losers. South can plan to ruff the club losers in dummy after drawing trump. Since the ♠Q is favorably located, declarer doesn't lose a trump trick and should finish with nine tricks . . . losing two hearts and two diamonds.

If East-West play in a diamond partscore, declarer has to lose two spade tricks and two club tricks. Whether declarer has to lose a heart trick depends on whether South leads hearts early enough to establish North's ♥Q as a winner. The defenders must do that before declarer can establish dummy's club suit on which to discard the heart losers.

Defense

There's nothing East-West can do to prevent North-South from taking nine tricks in a spade contract. As mentioned above, if East-West play in a diamond (or club) contract, South must lead hearts twice to establish North's ♥Q as a winner and hold declarer to eight tricks.

HAND: 2-4   NORTH
DEALER: WEST   ♠ Q 10 8 3
VUL: BOTH   ♥ A 9 3 2
                      ♦ 6
                      ♣ K J 7 6

WEST   EAST
♠ A 5   ♠ K 4
♥ J 8 7 5   ♥ Q 10 6
♦ K Q 5 2   ♦ J 8 7 4 3
♣ 8 3 2   ♣ A 10 4

                      SOUTH
                      ♠ J 9 7 6 2
                      ♥ K 4
                      ♦ A 10 9
                      ♣ Q 9 5

WEST	NORTH	EAST	SOUTH
Pass	Pass	Pass	1♠ (?)
Pass	3♠/4♠ (?)	Pass	Pass
Pass			

Bidding

None of the first three players really has enough to open the bidding. Even West, in third position, is unlikely to open light with such a poor diamond suit. That leaves everything up to South in fourth position. With only 10 high-card points, South may be tempted to pass the hand out and hope for a more exciting deal on the next hand. If South always passes with such hands, however, the partnership is going to miss a lot of partscore opportunities in the long run. Despite the 10 high-card points, the *Rule of 15* suggests that the South hand could be opened (10 high-card points + 5 spades = 15).

If South chooses to open 1♠, North may get excited. With the excellent spade support, North can revalue the hand using dummy points. 10 high-card points plus 3 dummy points for the singleton diamond makes the hand worth an opening bid.

Without conventional methods, it's difficult for North to describe such a strong hand opposite South's fourth chair opening bid. North can't afford to bid a new suit, 2♣ for example, because a new suit by responder is no longer forcing once you are a passed hand. In fact, if North does respond 2♣, South is likely to pass to avoid getting the partnership overboard. So, North may have to settle for the underbid of a limit raise to 3♠—leaving some leeway if South opened light—or the overbid of 4♠, hoping South has a full opening bid or more.

Whatever North chooses to bid, that's likely to end the auction since South was never planning to get beyond partscore with this particular hand.

Opening Lead

Against a spade contract, West will probably start with the ♦K, top of the touching high cards.

Play

Declarer starts with two spade losers, two diamond losers, and a club loser. The hand plays nicely for declarer since the missing spades are divided 2-2 and both diamond losers can be trumped in the North hand. Declarer loses only the ♠A-K and the ♣A, making ten tricks.

If North-South reach game on these combined hands they should consider themselves very lucky since the hands fit together quite perfectly. The deal does illustrate, however, that you might want to think twice before tossing in the cards with the South hand when there are three passes to you.

Defense

East-West can do no better than take their three top tricks against a spade contract. They can consider themselves quite unlucky if North-South reach a 'thin' game contract on these cards. On the other hand, they can consider themselves quite fortunate if the deal gets passed out.

PastTimes

> "Ely Culbertson, the bridge authority in the 1930's didn't believe that deceptive or obstructive bids belonged in the hands of the general public — although he was not above using such tactics himself! So, the weak two-bid came to an early end. Strong two-bids became the order of the day. In modern times, the weak two-bid is seen as part of standard bidding."
>
> —BETTER BRIDGE MAGAZINE, September 1998

Chapter Three

Obstructive Opening Bids

Obstructive bids designed to get in the way of the opponents are getting more attention in today's auctions. In addition to bidding constructively to your side's best contract, it's equally important to prevent the opponents from reaching their optimum spot. Bids that accomplish both objectives are especially useful and preemptive opening bids fall into that category.

Opening at a high level with less than the values for a one-level bid is risky business! It's often a good idea to bid more than you think you can make. You may push the opponents too high; you may make your contract through a favorable lie of the cards; or you may be defeated but lose less than if the opponents were allowed to play in their best contract. On the other hand, the opponents may double you and extract a large penalty. Preemptive opening bids require a delicate balance between aggressiveness and safety.

The value of hands with long suits is usually estimated using *playing tricks* instead of high-card and length points. Playing tricks are those you might reasonably expect to take if you buy the contract and name the trump suit. Compare these two hands.

1)	♠ A K 7	2)	♠ K Q J 10 9 8 7
	♥ A K 9		♥ 4
	♦ A K 8		♦ 10 3
	♣ 8 7 6 4		♣ 8 7 6

The first hand has 21 high-card points; the second has 6. Yet each is worth 6 *playing tricks.* There's no need to make an obstructive bid with the first hand. There's little chance the opponents will compete and you want to conserve the maximum bidding room to explore for the best contract. You might be able to make a game or slam in any of the four suits. The second hand, however, has little defensive value and will only be guaranteed of taking six tricks if you buy the contract and spades are the trump suit. This is the ideal hand for a preemptive opening bid, both describing the hand and obstructing the opponents.

Openings at the Three Level or Higher

Opening suit bids at the three level or higher are used to describe weak hands with a long suit. Although you are bidding more than you expect to make, the theory is that if you are doubled any penalty the opponents receive will be less than the value of the contract they could bid and make.

Three Level Preemptive Openings

> #### THREE-LEVEL PREEMPTIVE OPENING BID
> An opening bid of 3♣, 3♦, 3♥, or 3♠ shows a good seven-card suit and less than the values for a one-level opening bid.

1) ♠ 3
    ♥ K Q J 9 7 5 4
    ♦ 4 3
    ♣ 10 9 5

2) ♠ 6 5
    ♥ 2
    ♦ Q J 3
    ♣ A Q 10 9 7 5 4

The first hand can be opened 3♥; the second can be opened 3♣.

Four Level or Higher Preemptive Openings

> #### FOUR-LEVEL OR HIGHER PREEMPTIVE OPENING BID
> - With a weak hand and a good eight-card suit, open at the four level.
> - With a weak hand and a good nine-card suit, open at the game level in a major or minor.

1) ♠ A K J 10 8 7 6 3
    ♥ 7
    ♦ 9 2
    ♣ 8 3

2) ♠ 9 4
    ♥ —
    ♦ K Q J 9 8 6 5 4 3
    ♣ 10 5

The first hand can be opened 4♠; the second can be opened 5♦.

The Weak Two-Bid

Weak two-bids are an extension of preemptive opening bids. They've been around since the 1930's but weren't incorporated in most early bidding systems. They were thought to be a gadget for experts only. Eli Culbertson, one of the first promoters of the game, felt that the general public wasn't ready for them, even though he used the weak two-bid himself. Charles Goren had the same reservation about introducing this tactic to his readers.

As we move into the 21st century, however, the weak two-bid has become as popular as Blackwood and Stayman. Even if you don't plan to use weak two-bids in your partnership, you at least need to be familiar with them since they may be used by your opponents.

A weak two-bid can only be made in diamonds, hearts, or spades. The opening bid of 2♣ is reserved for all strong hands, as will be seen in the next chapter. The requirements for a weak two-bid are:

WEAK TWO-BID

An opening bid of 2♦, 2♥, or 2♠ shows a good six-card suit and 5-11 high-card points.

---

1) ♠ A K J 10 8 3   2) ♠ 8 6 5
     ♥ 7 4   ♥ Q J 8 7 4 2
     ♦ Q 7 6   ♦ Q 3
     ♣ 9 2   ♣ 8 5

The definition of 'good suit' is a matter of partnership style, vulnerability, and position at the table. The first hand would qualify as an opening 2♠ bid in most partnerships at any vulnerability in any position. Most players would not open the second hand 2♥, especially when vulnerable. Most of the strength should be concentrated in the six-card suit, typically with two of the top three honors or three of the top five.

Like preemptive opening bids at the three level or higher, the weak two bid serves as both an obstructive bid and as a good description of the hand for partner.

Examples

You are the dealer and your side is not vulnerable. You have to decide what call to make with each of the following hands.

♠ 4
♥ J 7 3
♦ A Q J 7 4 3 2
♣ 9 5

Open 3♦. There are only 8 high-card points but there is a good seven-card suit. Open at the three level. If the hand belongs to the opponents, your bid should present them with a challenge.

♠ A 9 5
♥ Q 7 6 5 4 3 2
♦ 3
♣ Q 9

Pass. You have a seven-card suit and you don't have enough to open the bidding at the one level. Your suit isn't very good, however, and it would be very risky to open at the three level.

♠ 10 8 2
♥ K Q J 8 7 5 4 3
♦ 5
♣ 6

Open 4♥. With a weak hand and a good eight-card suit, open at the four level. That makes it very difficult for the opponents to have a constructive auction if they have the majority of the strength.

♠ —
♥ 3
♦ 10 6 5
♣ K Q 10 9 7 5 4 3 2

Open 5♣. With a nine-card suit, open at the game level. In a minor, that means opening at the five level. It might seem dangerous, but the more clubs you have the worse your chance of taking any tricks on defense.

♠ K Q 10 9 7 5 4 3 2
♥ 3
♦ 10 6 5
♣ —

Open 4♠. With a nine-card major suit, open at the game level. You don't want to go past game in case, with a little help from partner, you can make exactly 10 tricks.

♠ 8 4
♥ K Q J 10 6 5
♦ K 9 5
♣ 7 3

Open 2♥. With a good six-card suit and a hand that isn't strong enough to open at the one level, you can open a weak two-bid . . . if that's the partnership style.

Improving Your Judgment

You don't have to open with a preemptive bid just because you have a long suit. It's an option. Your choice will depend on several factors.

1. The Rule of 500

When making a preempt you assume that if you are doubled and defeated, the penalty will not be greater than the value of the game the opponents could make. The value of a game, taking bonuses into account, is approximately 500 points. So, you can overbid by *two* tricks when vulnerable since the penalty would be 500 if doubled (200 for the first trick, 300 for the second). You can overbid by *three* tricks when non vulnerable since the penalty would still be only 500 if doubled (100 for the first trick, 200 for the second, and 200 for the third). This guideline is called the *Rule of Two and Three* or the *Rule of 500*.

RULE OF 500 (RULE OF TWO AND THREE)

When making a preemptive opening you can afford to:

- Overbid by two tricks when vulnerable.
- Overbid by three tricks when non vulnerable.

---

2. Playing Tricks

To estimate the number of playing tricks in a hand, assume the missing cards in your long suit will break reasonably evenly among the other three hands. Consider these two hands.

1)	♠	8 4	2)	♠	8 4 3
	♥	A Q J 8 6 5 3		♥	K Q 10 8 6 5
	♦	3		♦	3
	♣	9 4 2		♣	A 4 2

In the first hand, you can assume the 6 missing hearts are divided 2-2-2 around the table. You're still missing the ♥K, so you expect six playing tricks with hearts as trump. In the second hand, the missing hearts can be assumed to be divided 3-2-2 around the table. Since you are missing both the ♥A and ♥J, however, you only count four tricks in that suit, but can add one for the ♣A, bringing the total to five.

3. Offense, Not Defense

For an ideal preempt, the high cards should be concentrated in the long suit, not the side suits. The more high cards you have in other suit, the less likelihood the opponents can make anything and the riskier the preempt becomes. When it comes to weak two-bids, most players avoid hands with an outside four-card major or a void. It makes it too difficult to judge the value of the hand. Compare these two hands:

1)	♠ A K J 10 8 4	2)	♠ K J 9 7 5 3
	♥ 8 6		♥ K 10 7 4
	♦ 5 2		♦ —
	♣ 9 7 3		♣ K 8 2

With the concentrated strength in spades, the first hand is perfect for a weak 2♠ opening. The second hand has more high-card strength but is less than ideal for 2♠. The partnership might belong in hearts, and there's lots of defensive potential if the opponents come into the auction.

4. Position at the Table

When you are in first or second position, partner has yet to call and may have a good hand. A preemptive opening should be sound since it may be partner who has the strength. In third chair, you have more leeway. Partner has already passed, so you won't get in partner's way and the chance that the opponents have at least game has increased. This is the time to pull out the stops, occasionally preempting with a poor suit or one fewer card than normal. In fourth, there's no need to preempt since you can pass the hand out. You only open at the two level or higher with a 'super sound' preempt, which you expect to make.

1)	♠ 7	2)	♠ A Q J 10 8 7 4
	♥ J 9 8 6 5 4 3		♥ 4
	♦ K 9 5		♦ J 10 7 3
	♣ J 8		♣ 3

The first hand wouldn't be a sound preempt in first or second seat with such a poor suit. In third, especially non vulnerable, you might bend the rules and open 3♥. The second hand would be a sound preempt in first or second, and you might even open 3♠ in fourth. In third, you might try putting extra pressure on the opponents by opening 4♠.

Summary

Preemptive Opening Bids

A preemptive opening bid at the three level (3♣, 3♦, 3♥, or 3♠) shows:

- a long, strong suit, typically seven cards in length;
- a weak hand, less than the values for a one-level opening bid

With a longer suit, you can open at a higher level:

- with a weak hand and a good eight-card suit, open at the four level.
- with a weak hand and a good nine-card suit, open at the game level.

If the partnership uses weak two-bids, all strong hands are opened 2♣, and an opening bid of 2♦, 2♥, or 2♠ shows:

- a good six-card suit;
- a weak hand, typically 5-11 high-card points.

The decision on whether to open with a preemptive bid depends on partnership style, vulnerability, and position at the table. The hand is usually evaluated in terms of *playing tricks* and should meet the *Rule of 500*—down two tricks vulnerable, down three tricks non vulnerable.

In third position, and when non vulnerable against vulnerable opponents, you can afford to be more aggressive in preemptive openings, occasionally bidding with a weaker or shorter suit than would be required in first or second position.

Quiz

1. Neither side is vulnerable and you are the dealer. What call do you make on the following hands?

a) ♠ 9 4
   ♥ 3
   ♦ 10 4 3
   ♣ K Q J 9 6 4 2

b) ♠ 6 3
   ♥ A K 10 9 7 3
   ♦ 10 9 6 4
   ♣ 8

c) ♠ J 8 6 5 4 3 2
   ♥ K Q 5
   ♦ 7
   ♣ Q 3

d) ♠ 6 3
   ♥ A K J 10 7 5 3 2
   ♦ 8
   ♣ 10 8

e) ♠ K J 4
   ♥ 3
   ♦ A Q J 9 7 5 2
   ♣ J 5

f) ♠ K Q 10 8 4 3
   ♥ 7
   ♦ Q J 5
   ♣ 9 4 2

g) ♠ —
   ♥ 6
   ♦ 7 6 3
   ♣ A K J 9 8 7 5 3 2

h) ♠ Q 8 5 3
   ♥ A Q J 8 7 3
   ♦ —
   ♣ 9 4 2

i) ♠ 7 4
   ♥ K 9 5
   ♦ 8 2
   ♣ A J 10 8 4 2

2. The opponents are vulnerable you are not. What call do you make with the following hands after two passes to you in third chair?

a) ♠ K J 10 9 7 4 3
   ♥ 7
   ♦ J 9 3
   ♣ 10 6

b) ♠ 8 3
   ♥ A K J 9 7 3
   ♦ Q J 4
   ♣ 7 4

c) ♠ 5
   ♥ 10 3
   ♦ J 9 6 4
   ♣ A K J 10 8 3

d) ♠ Q 5
   ♥ 6
   ♦ K Q 10 9 7 6 3 2
   ♣ 5 2

e) ♠ Q 7 3
   ♥ Q 8 7 5 4 2
   ♦ K 5
   ♣ 9 2

f) ♠ A K J 10 7
   ♥ K 7 3
   ♦ 10 7 4
   ♣ 9 4

g) ♠ 2
   ♥ 7 5
   ♦ Q 10 9 7 6 5 3
   ♣ 10 4 2

h) ♠ 5
   ♥ A K Q 8 7 5 3
   ♦ 10 9 8 6
   ♣ 9

i) ♠ K Q J 10 8
   ♥ 7 4
   ♦ 10 3
   ♣ 9 7 4 2

Answers to Quiz

1a) 3♣. A good seven-card suit and only 6 high-card points. Ideal for a non vulnerable three-level preemptive opening.

1b) 2♥. With a good six-card suit you can open a weak two-bid.

1c) Pass. With a poor suit and high cards outside of spades, this would not be a sound preemptive opening in first or second position.

1d) 4♥. With a good eight-card suit and no outside strength, open at the four level. This would be a good choice even when vulnerable.

1e) 1♦. You have a good seven-card suit but enough strength to open at the one level. No need to take away your side's bidding room.

1f) 2♠. An opening weak two-bid will describe the hand nicely . . . a good six-card suit and 5-11 points.

1g) 5♣. With a nine-card suit open at the game level.

1h) Pass. Most partnerships avoid weak two-bids with four-card support for an outside major or with a void. Here you have both.

1i) Pass. You can't open a weak two-bid in clubs and the suit isn't long or strong enough for a three level preempt in first or second position.

2a) 3♠. With a decent seven-card suit, open at the three level in third position. It would be a little riskier if your side were vulnerable.

2b) 1♥/2♥. You have enough to open at the one level but, in third chair, you might choose a weak two-bid for tactical reasons.

2c) 3♣. You can't open a weak two-bid in clubs, but you might try a three-level preempt in third chair with a good six-card suit.

2d) 4♦. A weak hand, a good eight-card suit, and partner has already passed. Time to put the maximum pressure on the opponents.

2e) Pass (2♥). Some players might open this hand with a weak two-bid in third chair but, with such a poor suit, you could get into trouble.

2f) 1♠. This hand can be treated as a light opening bid in third chair.

2g) 3♦ (Pass). The suit isn't that great and you might suffer a large penalty. On the other hand, partner has passed, so the opponents very likely have a game or slam. Some players would take the risk.

2h) 4♥ (3♥). Now that partner is a passed hand, opening 4♥ would be a reasonable shot. It might even make!

2i) 2♠ (Pass). Third chair, non vulnerable, opposite a passed partner. Perhaps this is the time to treat that five-card suit as a six-card suit.

HAND: 3-1
DEALER: NORTH
VUL: NONE

NORTH
♠ A K 6 3
♥ 6
♦ Q 10 5
♣ J 9 7 3 2

WEST
♠ Q 7 5
♥ 10 2
♦ A 8 4 3
♣ A K 10 8

EAST
♠ J 10 9
♥ A 4
♦ K 9 7 2
♣ Q 6 5 4

SOUTH
♠ 8 4 2
♥ K Q J 9 8 7 5 3
♦ J 6
♣ —

WEST	NORTH	EAST	SOUTH
	Pass	Pass	4♥
Pass	Pass	Pass	

Bidding

After two passes, the bidding comes to South in third chair. South doesn't have enough to open the bidding at the one level but has a fine heart suit that should be worth about seven playing tricks. With an eight-card suit, South can describe the hand with a preemptive opening of 4♥. That's in line with the *Rule of 500*. Non vulnerable, the worst that can happen is that South could be doubled and defeated three tricks for a penalty of 500 points. If partner's hand is also weak, East-West can likely make at least a game contract.

On this hand, the 4♥ bid is likely to buy the contract. West has enough to open at the one level, but not enough to come into the auction at the four level, especially since partner has already passed. Most partnerships would play a double by West as *cooperative*—showing enough high-card strength to likely defeat the contract but allowing partner to take out to a long suit with a good playing hand. On this hand, West may find that a double doesn't work very well.

Opening Lead

West is on lead against the 4♥ contract and will start with the ♣A, top of the touching high cards.

Play

South has a spade loser, a heart loser, and two diamond losers. There's not much that can be done about the heart and diamond losers, so declarer should focus on eliminating the spade loser. Declarer's plan should be to promote a winner in the diamond suit by driving out the defenders' ♦A and ♦K.

After ruffing the opening club lead, South should waste no time before going after the diamonds. The extra diamond winner must be established before the defenders can set up a spade winner. South should lead the ♦J. Either defender can win this trick and lead a spade, but declarer is a step ahead. Declarer can win the spade trick and lead a high diamond from dummy to drive out the defenders remaining high card. If they lead another spade, declarer wins in the North hand to play the established diamond winner and discard the spade loser from the South hand.

Now it's safe to start drawing trump. Declarer loses a heart and two diamond tricks, but that's all.

Defense

If declarer ruffs the first club trick and immediately leads a trump, the defenders have a chance. East should win ♥A and lead a spade. East can see that the defenders have no tricks coming from the club suit and at most two tricks from the diamond suit. They will need to develop a spade winner to go along with the ♥A. If declarer wins the spade and leads a diamond from dummy, the defender who wins this trick should lead another spade, establish a trick in the suit. When they later win a second diamond trick, they can take the spade winner to defeat the contract.

Of course, West could always defeat the contract by leading a spade initially, instead of a high club. That requires a high degree of clairvoyance, however . . . or a peek at the full deal beforehand!

HAND: 3-2
DEALER: EAST
VUL: N-S

NORTH
♠ K 8 4
♥ A 7 6
♦ Q 5 3
♣ A 8 4 3

WEST
♠ Q 7 2
♥ K Q 8 5 2
♦ 4
♣ K 9 5 2

EAST
♠ J 10 5
♥ 10 3
♦ A K J 10 8 6 2
♣ 6

SOUTH
♠ A 9 6 3
♥ J 9 4
♦ 9 7
♣ Q J 10 7

WEST	NORTH	EAST	SOUTH
		3♦	Pass
Pass	Pass		

Bidding

Non vulnerable in first chair, East has an ideal preemptive opening bid of 3♦. Not only does this describe the hand nicely to partner, it will also present a challenge to the opponents to get into the auction if the hand belongs to them.

South doesn't have enough to compete for the contract. West may not be happy with diamonds as the trump suit but should not attempt to 'improve' the contract. Any bid West makes could get the partnership into worse trouble. Besides, East has described a hand that will only take a lot of tricks if the trump suit is diamonds.

North has a one-level opening bid, but it would be very dangerous to enter the auction at the three level, especially when vulnerable. North should accept that the preemptive bid has done its job and go quietly, hoping to defeat the contract.

Opening Lead

Against the 3♦ contract, South could start with the ♣Q, top of the three-card sequence.

Play

East has two sure losers in spades, one in hearts, and one in clubs. To make the contract, East will have to avoid a diamond loser. With eight diamonds in the combined hands, the percentage play is to take a finesse for the missing ♦Q rather than playing the ♦A-K hoping the ♦Q will fall—*eight ever, nine never* (with eight combined cards missing the queen, take the finesse; with nine combined cards missing the queen, play the ace and king hoping the queen will fall).

To take the diamond finesse, declarer needs an entry to dummy. There is no immediate entry, so declarer will have to create one in the heart suit. If the defenders begin by leading two rounds of clubs, East can ruff the second trick and lead a heart to dummy's ♥Q. North can win the ♥A and the defenders can take their two spade winners, but they can't prevent declarer from regaining the lead and reaching dummy with the ♥K. The ♦4 is led from dummy and, when North follows with a low diamond, declarer plays the ♦10 or ♦J, taking the finesse. When that works, declare continues with the ♦A and ♦K. The ♦Q falls on the third round and East makes the contract.

Defense

There's nothing the defenders can do to prevent declarer from making nine tricks with diamonds as trumps.

HAND: 3-3
DEALER: SOUTH
VUL: E-W

NORTH
♠ 7 6 4
♥ J 8 3
♦ 4
♣ K Q J 9 8 3

WEST
♠ K 5 3
♥ A 9 4
♦ K 8 7 5 2
♣ 5 2

EAST
♠ Q 9 2
♥ K 7 6
♦ A Q J 9 6
♣ A 10

SOUTH
♠ A J 10 8
♥ Q 10 5 2
♦ 10 3
♣ 7 6 4

WEST	NORTH	EAST	SOUTH
			Pass
Pass	3♣ (?)	3NT (?)	Pass
Pass	Pass		

Bidding

After South and West pass, North has to decide what to do in third chair. North doesn't have the right type of hand to open 1♣ and can't open 2♣, since that would show a strong hand.

An opening bid of 3♣ typically promises a seven-card suit. In third chair, non vulnerable, North can exercise some judgment. Partner has already passed, showing fewer than 13 points. Since North doesn't hold much in the way of high cards, it's quite likely that East-West have at least a game contract. Left to their own devices, they may well find their best spot. An opening preemptive bid of 3♣, however, may make their task more challenging. It's possible that the opponents might double and extract a large penalty, but the risk is worth taking.

If North passes, East-West have an easy time getting to their best spot. East opens 1NT and West raises to 3NT. If South leads anything except a club, that contract will roll home with nine tricks.

If, instead, North opens 3♣, East is faced with an uncomfortable choice. East might overcall 3♦—in which case the partnership might get to 5♦, which has little chance. East might make a takeout double—which is again likely to lead to a diamond contract. Or, East might overcall 3NT, hoping to find enough strength in the West hand to take nine tricks. That's probably the best choice—even though it doesn't prove successful on this particular hand.

Opening Lead

If North doesn't open the bidding and East-West reach 3NT, South would probably lead the ♠J, top of the *interior sequence*. That would allow East-West to take at least nine tricks, likely ten.

If North opens 3♣ and East becomes declarer in 3NT, South would have a difficult time justifying any lead other than a club. The lead from three low clubs in partner's suit depends on the partnership style. Some partnerships prefer a low club, some prefer *top of nothing*, some prefer the middle card, intending to following with the top card, and then the low card—*MUD* (middle, up, down). Whatever the partnership style, a club lead works best for the defenders.

Play

In 3NT, East is unlikely to succeed after a club lead. East can hold up one round with the ♣A but will have to win the second round. There are only eight top tricks and a ninth trick can only come from the spade suit.

East can hope that North started with a seven-card club suit, leaving South with no more. East might try sneaking through a spade trick early by leading a low spade toward dummy, but South should hop up with the ♠A and lead another club to defeat the contract by three tricks. Perhaps East should just settle for eight tricks.

Defense

As long as South holds on to a club and takes the ♠A when given a chance, the defenders should be able to defeat 3NT. If East-West land in a diamond contract, careful defense will give the defenders two spade tricks, a heart trick and a club trick.

HAND: 3-4
DEALER: WEST
VUL: BOTH

NORTH
♠ 9 8 4
♥ K J
♦ K 10 6 4
♣ K J 10 8

WEST
♠ A Q J 10 7 5
♥ 10 5 2
♦ Q 5 2
♣ 4

EAST
♠ K 3
♥ A 9 7 4 3
♦ J 7 3
♣ Q 9 5

SOUTH
♠ 6 2
♥ Q 8 6
♦ A 9 8
♣ A 7 6 3 2

WEST	NORTH	EAST	SOUTH
2♠	Pass	Pass	Pass

Bidding

West doesn't have enough to open the bidding at the one level, and a three-level preemptive bid would be very risky with only a six-card suit when vulnerable. Still, the hand has at least five playing tricks with spades as trump, so West would like to mention the suit.

If the partnership plays *weak two-bids*, West can describe the hand nicely by opening 2♠. If West does open 2♠, that's likely to buy the contract. Neither North nor South has enough to enter the auction at the three level, even though North-South might make a partscore in clubs. East has no reason to bid any more since West is showing less than the values for an opening bid.

Opening Lead

Against a 2♠ contract, North has a difficult choice of leads. The ♣J, top of the *interior sequence*, is a reasonable choice.

Play

In 2♠, there are two heart losers, three potential diamond losers, and a club loser. West could hope to avoid a diamond loser by leading toward one of the honors, hoping a defender was dealt both the ♦A and ♦K. A better alternative, however, is to try to establish extra winners in the heart suit on which to discard at least one diamond loser.

Suppose the defenders lead two rounds of clubs. West can trump the second trick and play three rounds of spades to draw the missing trumps. Declarer should be careful not to discard a heart from dummy on the third spade. Next, West leads a heart, but plays *low* cards from both hands, giving up a trick to the defenders. Declarer can't afford to use dummy's ♥A too early, since it's the only sure entry to the dummy.

At this point, it won't do the defenders any good to take their ♦A and ♦K. If they do, they will make declarer's task easy, since the ♦Q will be established as a winner. Instead, they may lead another club. West ruffs, and again plays a low heart from both hands, giving the defenders their second trick in the suit. Now the defense has no winning answer. If they lead a club, declarer can ruff, cross to dummy's ♥A, and play two more winning hearts, discarding diamond losers. Declarer will make an overtrick. If the defenders take their diamond winners, they establish a diamond trick for West, and the contract is still made.

Defense

The defenders cannot defeat the contract if declarer takes the recommended line of play. The best they can do is hold West to eight tricks. If declarer doesn't go after the hearts, however, they have a chance. They should continue leading clubs, waiting for declarer to play the diamond suit. If declarer leads diamonds, the defenders can get three tricks in the suit and defeat the contract.

The diamond suit on this hand is referred to as a *frozen suit.* Whoever breaks the ice by leading diamonds gives up a trick to the other side. Recognizing *frozen suits* is important for both declarer and the defenders. Whether contracts are made or defeated will often depend on which side is forced to lead such a suit.

> *"If you intend to pass your partner's forcing bid, it's best to drive to the bridge game in separate cars."*
>
> —BETTER BRIDGE TIP

Chapter Four

Strong Opening Bids

Some hands have so much strength that they are likely to make game opposite little or no strength from partner. For example:

♠ 8
♥ A K Q J 8 6 5
♦ A 6
♣ A K 5

You can expect to take ten tricks with hearts as trump even if partner has no points and no hearts. If you open 1♥, there is the possibility that partner will pass and you'll miss a game. If you open 4♥, you haven't left much room to explore for slam. If partner has as little as the ♦K and ♣Q, you can take twelve tricks.

Such hands were traditionally opened with a *strong two-bid*, 2♥. This was forcing—so partner couldn't pass—and left room to look for slam. With the advent of *weak two-bids*, however, opening bids of 2♦, 2♥, and 2♠ are no longer used to show strong hands. Instead, all strong hands of about 22 or more points are opened with an *artificial 2♣ bid*.

The opening 2♣ bid says nothing about clubs, it is merely a forcing bid. Responder must say something. Unless responder has a good five-card or longer suit with about 8 or more points, responder usually makes a *waiting response of 2♦*. This leaves the maximum amount of room for opener to describe the hand.

With the above hand, opener would start with 2♣ and rebid 2♥ over the 2♦ response. There's no need for opener to jump, since the 2♥ rebid is now forcing. It's just as though opener had started with a strong two-bid in hearts. No extra room has been used when opener has a strong two-bid in a major suit. Only with a minor suit will opener have to show the "real" suit at the three level.

Most partnerships agree responder shows a very bad hand by rebidding 2NT—similar to the 'old-fashioned' negative response to a strong two-bid. You could now bid 4♥ with this hand, confident that the partnership does not have a slam.

Opening Strong Balanced Hands

Using the artificial 2♣ opening with strong hands of 22 or more points affects the ranges used for showing balanced hands. Here's the complete structure:

	OPENING BALANCED HANDS
0 – 11/12	Pass.
12/13 – 14	Open one-of-a-suit planning to rebid notrump at the cheapest available level.
15 – 17	Open 1NT.
18 – 19	Open one-of-a-suit planning to rebid notrump jumping a level.
20 – 21	Open 2NT.
22 – 24	Open 2♣ planning to rebid 2NT.
25 – 27	Open 2♣ planning to rebid 3NT.
28 – 30	Open 2♣ planning to rebid 4NT.

1)   ♠ K J 8   2)   ♠ A J 7 5
     ♥ A Q 9   ♥ K J 10 4
     ♦ K Q 7 5   ♦ A Q
     ♣ A J 6   ♣ A K 10

The first hand would be opened 2NT, showing a balanced hand of 20–21 points. This is not forcing and partner could pass. The second would be opened 2♣. Responder bids 2♦, waiting to hear more about your hand. You rebid 2NT showing a balanced hand of 22–24 points. This is not forcing and responder could pass with a very weak hand.

On both hands, responder can use the partnership's standard methods following opener's 2NT bid. 3♣ would be the Stayman convention, for example, asking opener to show a four-card major suit.

An opening bid of 3NT is no longer used to show a strong balanced hand. Instead, it can be assigned another meaning by the partnership.

Opening Strong Unbalanced Hands

If opener rebids a suit rather than notrump after opening 2♣, that is still a forcing bid. The style for some partnerships is that the auction must then continue until at least game is reached. A more common agreement is that, if responder makes a negative 2NT rebid and opener merely rebids a major suit at the three level, responder can pass. If opener shows a second suit, responder must keep the bidding going to at least game.

1) ♠ A Q 9   2) ♠ A K J 9 6
    ♥ A K Q J 8 5   ♥ A K Q 8 2
    ♦ K Q 6   ♦ 3
    ♣ J   ♣ A J

On the first hand, opener bids 2♣ and responder bids 2♦. Opener now shows the strong two-bid in hearts by bidding 2♥. If responder now makes the negative rebid of 2NT, opener's rebid of 3♥ isn't forcing. Responder can pass with a very weak hand.

On the second hand, opener also bids 2♣ and gets a 2♦ waiting response from partner. The guidelines when you have a choice of suits to show are the same as when opening at the one level. Opener rebids 2♠, the higher-ranking of the two five-card suits. If responder makes the negative rebid of 2NT, opener shows the second suit by bidding 3♥. Responder can't pass this bid, even with no points, since the partnership is now committed to the game level.

If responder makes a positive bid—either immediately in response to the 2♣ opening or after hearing opener's rebid—the partnership is committed to the game level. If responder raises opener's suit, for example, the partnership is headed for at least game and perhaps a slam. Once the trump suit has been agreed, the partnership's normal slam bidding methods—such as Blackwood and cue-bids—come into effect.

Since a raise of opener's suit is forcing, responder can show support for opener's suit with a very weak hand by jumping directly to the game level. On the first hand, for example, responder's jump to 4♥ over opener's 2♥ rebid would say, "I have support for your hearts but nothing else that would be of any value . . . no ace, no king, no singleton, and no void. If you want to bid slam you're on your own."

Examples

What opening call would you make with each of the following hands?
What do you plan to do next?

♠ A J 9 4　　Open 2NT, showing a balanced hand of 20-21
♥ K J 7 3　　points. If partner responds 3♣, the Stayman con-
♦ A K Q　　 vention, you will bid 3♥ showing the four- card
♣ K 4　　　 heart suit . . . bidding the major suits 'up the line.'

♠ A K 4　　 Open 2♣. If partner responds 2♦, you will rebid
♥ Q J 7　　 2NT, showing a balanced hand of 22-24 points. If
♦ A J 3　　 partner then bids 3♣, you will bid 3♦ showing no
♣ A K J 5　 four-card major suit.

♠ A K 10 8　Open 2♣. If partner responds 2♦, rebid 3NT,
♥ K Q J　　 showing a balanced hand of 25-27 points. Most
♦ A Q J　　 partnerships don't have many agreements after
♣ A K 8　　 this start because such hands occur so infrequently.

♠ A Q　　　 Open 2♣. If partner responds 2♦, you plan to
♥ A K Q 9 8　rebid 2♥, showing a strong two-bid in hearts. If
♦ 3　　　　 partner then bids 2NT, showing a weak hand, you
♣ A K J 10 5 can show the second suit by bidding 3♣. That's
　　　　　　 forcing and the next move is up to partner.

♠ A Q J 9 8 3　Open 2♣. If partner responds 2♦, rebid 2♠ to
♥ Q　　　　 show the strong two-bid. If partner bids 2NT, you
♦ A Q J　　 can rebid 3♠. This is not forcing, so partner can
♣ A Q 5　　 pass with nothing of value.

♠ Q 4　　　 Open 2♣. If partner responds 2♦, rebid 3♦,
♥ A K J　　 showing a strong 'two-bid' in diamonds. A
♦ A K J 9 8 7 3 disadvantage of the artificial 2♣ opening is that you
♣ A　　　　 can't show your minor suit below the three level.

Improving Your Judgment

The guideline for opening 2♣ is about 22 or more points. However, it isn't just the high cards that determine your opening bid.

1. Offensive Tricks

A good measure of an unbalanced hand is the number of playing tricks the hand is likely to take. Ideally, you should be within one trick of game before opening 2♣. Consider these two hands.

1)	♠ A Q 8 4	2)	♠ A K Q 10 9 3
	♥ Q		♥ A K Q 4
	♦ A K Q		♦ 3
	♣ A J 8 4 3		♣ 4 2

The first hand has 22 high-card points plus 1 length point. There are only five sure tricks, however, and it wouldn't be a good idea to open 2♣. If partner bids 2♦, you don't want to rebid 3♣ with such a meager suit. Open 1♣. If partner can't respond over that, it's unlikely your side has a game.

The second hand has only 18 high-card points plus 2 length points for the six-card suit, but it's a much better hand to open 2♣. If the missing spades and hearts are reasonably evenly divided among the other three hands, you can likely take ten tricks with no high-card help from partner.

2. Defensive Tricks

To open 2♣, you should have some aces and kings that will take tricks even if you are defending. Compare these hands.

1)	♠ A	2)	♠ —
	♥ A K 10 8 7 4		♥ K Q J 10 8 7 6 5
	♦ A K J 4		♦ Q J 10 9 7
	♣ K 4		♣ —

The first hand has lots of offensive potential but also some defensive potential if the opponents were to compete in spades or clubs. It should be opened 2♣. On the second hand, you can take ten tricks by yourself if allowed to play in a heart contract. But you have no sure trick on defense if the opponents compete in spades or clubs. Don't open 2♣. Open 1♥ or 4♥ and try to buy the contract at a suitable level.

3. 4-4-4-1 Hands

Strong hands with 4-4-4-1 distribution are very awkward to bid. Because of the singleton, you can't really treat them as balanced, but with no five-card suit, they aren't really unbalanced. You may need to go slowly to find a fit. Look at these two hands:

1)	♠ A Q J 8	2)	♠ A K 5 3
	♥ A Q 8 4		♥ A
	♦ J		♦ A Q J 4
	♣ A K J 4		♣ A Q 8 3

Despite the 22 high-card points in the first hand, the bidding is likely to become awkward if you open 2♣ since there is no suitable rebid. Open 1♣ and hope partner responds. On the second hand, you have a similar challenge with 24 high-card points. Most players would open 2♣ anyway, treating the hand as balanced and rebidding 2NT after a 2♦ response.

4. Balanced Judgment

Be prepared to exercise some judgment with your opening bid and rebid when dealing with strong hands. Consider these two hands:

1)	♠ K Q 10	2)	♠ A K J
	♥ A J		♥ K 5
	♦ A J 10 9 8		♦ K 4
	♣ A Q 10		♣ A K Q 8 7 5

The first hand has only 21 high-card points but is worth an opening 2♣ bid. It has a five-card suit and no card lower than an eight. Treat it as a balanced hand of 22-24 points and rebid 2NT over a 2♦ response.

With 23 high-card points plus 2 length points for the six-card suit, the second hand should definitely be opened 2♣. If partner responds 2♦, a rebid of 3♣ may leave partner awkwardly placed with a very weak hand. If partner bids 3NT, you will have to put your hand down as dummy. A heart or diamond opening lead may trap your king and allow the defenders to take enough tricks to defeat the contract. A more practical rebid is 3NT, treating the hand as balanced with 25-27 points. If the opening lead is a heart or a diamond from your left, you should easily be able to take nine tricks.

Summary

Strong Opening Bids

Balanced Hands

- 20 – 21   Open 2NT.
- 22 – 24   Open 2♣ planning to rebid 2NT.
- 25 – 27   Open 2♣ planning to rebid 3NT.

Unbalanced Hands

- 22 or more   Open 2♣. This is a strong artificial forcing bid.

When partner opens 2♣, responder usually makes an artificial *waiting response* of 2♦, leaving opener room to describe the hand.

Keep the following points in mind:

- When opener shows a balanced hand, responder is not forced to bid again. Responder can use the standard partnership methods after a notrump opening bid.
- When opener shows an unbalanced hand, responder is forced to bid again. With a very weak hand, responder bids notrump at the cheapest available level.
- If opener rebids the original major suit at the three level after responder has shown a weak hand, responder can pass. Any other rebid by opener or responder commits the partnership to the game level.

Quiz

1. You are the dealer with both sides vulnerable. What is your opening call with each of the following hands?

a) ♠ K J 8
   ♥ A Q 8 3
   ♦ K 4
   ♣ A Q J 9

b) ♠ K Q 7
   ♥ A K J
   ♦ A J 8 4
   ♣ A J 10

c) ♠ A K J 10 9 7 4
   ♥ A K J
   ♦ K Q
   ♣ 3

d) ♠ A K 8 5
   ♥ A Q
   ♦ A K Q 8
   ♣ K Q 7

e) ♠ 10 5
   ♥ A K Q 10 8 3
   ♦ A K Q 9
   ♣ 8

f) ♠ K Q 8 5
   ♥ K
   ♦ K J 6 5 2
   ♣ A K Q

g) ♠ A K 5
   ♥ K 4
   ♦ A Q J 8 7
   ♣ Q 10 5

h) ♠ A K 7 5
   ♥ A Q J 3
   ♦ 4
   ♣ A K J 4

i) ♠ K Q J 9 8 7 6
   ♥ —
   ♦ K Q J 10 4
   ♣ 7

2. You open the bidding 2♣ and partner responds with a waiting bid of 2♦. What's your rebid with each of the following hands?

a) ♠ K Q 10 8
   ♥ A K Q
   ♦ J 9
   ♣ A Q J 7

b) ♠ —
   ♥ A K Q 5
   ♦ A 8 5
   ♣ A K J 9 8 3

c) ♠ A J
   ♥ K Q J 8
   ♦ A K Q 7
   ♣ A J 3

d) ♠ K Q
   ♥ A K Q J 9 7 6
   ♦ —
   ♣ A K 8 3

e) ♠ 4
   ♥ A K 5
   ♦ A K J 10 8 7 3
   ♣ A J

f) ♠ A Q
   ♥ K Q 9
   ♦ A 9 3
   ♣ A Q J 8 4

g) ♠ A K J 8 3
   ♥ A
   ♦ 3
   ♣ A K J 9 5 4

h) ♠ A K
   ♥ K 3
   ♦ A K Q 8 6 3
   ♣ K J 5

i) ♠ A K
   ♥ K Q J 4
   ♦ K Q J
   ♣ A K Q J

Answers to Quiz

1a) 2NT. This shows a balanced hand of 20-21 points when the partnership uses the 2♣ opening for all strong hands.

1b) 2♣. With a balanced hand and 23 high-card points, open the bidding 2♣. The hand is too strong to open 2NT.

1c) 2♣. With 21 high-card points and a strong seven-card suit, open with 2♣, planning to show a strong two-bid in spades.

1d) 2♣. This is an old-fashioned 3NT opening bid, showing 25-27 points. Playing weak two-bids, however, this hand is opened 2♣.

1e) 2♣. There are only 18 high-card points but you can expect to take ten tricks in hearts with almost no help from partner.

1f) 1♦. Lots of points but they aren't working well together. This hand isn't balanced and isn't a strong two-bid in diamonds. Start slowly.

1g) 2NT. 19 high-card points plus 1 for the five-card suit make this hand worth a 2NT opening bid.

1h) 1♣. Despite all the points, you don't have a strong two-bid in any suit. If partner can't bid over 1♣ it's unlikely you have a game.

1i) 1♠ (4♠). You can take ten tricks in your own hand but don't have a single sure trick on defense, so this hand doesn't qualify as a strong two-bid. The hand won't get passed out if you open 1♠.

2a) 2NT. This shows a balanced hand with 22-24 points. Don't worry about the lack of a sure stopper in diamonds.

2b) 3♣. Your original 2♣ bid said nothing about clubs. You have to rebid 3♣ to show your suit. You plan to show hearts next.

2c) 3NT. This rebid shows a balanced hand with 25-27 points.

2d) 2♥. There's no need to jump to game with this hand. The 2♥ rebid is forcing. Leave lots of room to explore for slam.

2e) 3♦. Show your suit. Partner may become declarer in diamonds!

2f) 2NT. The hand is balanced with 22 high-card points and 1 for length.

2g) 3♣. Show the longer suit first. Bid and rebid the spades later.

2h) 3NT (3♦). Treat this as a strong balanced hand. If you rebid 3♦, partner may be awkwardly placed. 3NT is more likely to be successful with your hand as declarer rather than the dummy.

2i) 4NT. You should be so lucky! This shows a balanced hand of 28-30 points and is not forcing . . . and doesn't ask for aces.

HAND: 4-1   NORTH
DEALER: NORTH   ♠ K J 9 4
VUL: NONE   ♥ K Q 9
                          ♦ A K 7
                          ♣ A 7 3

WEST   EAST
♠ 8 7 5 2   ♠ 6 3
♥ 5 4 2   ♥ 8 7 6 3
♦ 3   ♦ Q 9 6 5
♣ K Q 10 9 8   ♣ 5 4 2

                          SOUTH
                          ♠ A Q 10
                          ♥ A J 10
                          ♦ J 10 8 4 2
                          ♣ J 6

WEST	NORTH	EAST	SOUTH
	2NT	Pass	6NT
Pass	Pass	Pass	

Bidding

With a balanced hand and 20 high-card points, North opens the bidding 2NT. When the partnership uses 2♣ as a strong artificial opening bid, then an opening bid of 2NT is commonly used to show 20-21 points. With 22 or more, you open 2♣ and rebid in notrump.

South has 13 high-card points plus 1 for the five-card suit. There should be enough combined strength for a small slam, but not enough for a grand slam. South should keep things simple by raising directly to 6NT. A raise to 4NT would be *quantitative* (invitational), not Blackwood, and North might pass with 'only' 20 points. To ask for aces directly over a notrump opening bid, the Gerber convention is used, 4♣.

There's no need to ask for aces, since the partnership cannot be missing two aces with 33 or more combined high-card points. Whether the partnership has all the aces, or is missing an ace, the final contract should still be 6NT.

Opening Lead

With no indication from the auction, East will likely lead the ♦5, fourth best, or a more passive heart.

If South bid a conventional 4♣ during the auction, West might make a lead-directing double. If that happens, East would makethe winning club lead for the defense.

Play

On any lead except a club, North has an easy time developing twelve tricks. There are four sure tricks in spades, three in hearts, two in diamonds, and one in clubs. Two more tricks can be developed in the diamond suit by playing the ♦A, ♦K and giving up a tricks to East's ♦Q.

On a club lead, declarer is in trouble. As the cards lie, there's no way to develop more than 10 tricks without giving up a trick to East's ♦Q, and the defenders can then take their club tricks.

Defense

The defenders are unlikely to find the winning club lead, unless East is very inspired or North-South give West a chance to double clubs during the auction. If South does bid clubs, West should double, asking East to lead the suit. It's the only suit West wants led, and it's highly unlikely East will lead a club if West remains silent throughout the auction.

There's no need for North-South to give East-West any chance to exchange information during the bidding. Sometimes, a quick auction to the desired spot will bring unexpected benefits.

HAND: 4-2
DEALER: EAST
VUL: N-S

NORTH
♠ 10 8 4 2
♥ Q 10 7 4 3
♦ K 6
♣ Q 8

WEST
♠ A K J
♥ A 9 5
♦ A Q
♣ A J 6 4 3

EAST
♠ Q 7 6 3
♥ 8 6 2
♦ 10 7 5
♣ K 5 2

SOUTH
♠ 9 5
♥ K J
♦ J 9 8 4 3 2
♣ 10 9 7

WEST	NORTH	EAST	SOUTH
		Pass	Pass
2♣	Pass	2♦	Pass
2NT	Pass	3♣	Pass
3♦	Pass	3NT	Pass
Pass	Pass		

Bidding

With 23 high-card points plus 1 length point for the five-card club suit, West is too strong for an opening bid of 2NT if the partnership range is 20–21. Instead, West starts with an artificial 2♣ opening. With only 5 points, East makes a *waiting* response of 2♦ ... waiting to hear what West has to say next. West finishes the description of the hand by rebidding 2NT, showing a balanced hand of 22–24 points.

With 5 points, East has enough to take the partnership to game. East can use the same methods as the partnership normally uses over a 2NT opening bid. This is likely to include 3♣ as the Stayman convention, asking if opener has a four-card major suit. When opener denies holding a four-card major with the 3♦ bid, East settles for game in notrump.

Opening Lead

Against 3NT, North will start with the ♥4, fourth highest from longest and strongest.

Play

Declarer can count four sure tricks in spades, one in hearts, one in diamonds, and two in clubs. One more trick is needed. This might come from a successful diamond finesse for the missing ♦K or, perhaps, a successful club finesse for the missing ♣Q.

One challenge is that the defenders may be able to establish enough heart tricks to defeat the contract, especially if the lead is lost to North. Declarer should start by *holding up* with the ♥A, and holding up a second time when the suit is continued. On the third round of hearts, West must win the ♥A, but now it is only North who is the dangerous opponent. It's safe to lose a trick to South.

West should take the three top spade tricks to *unblock* the suit. Rather than staking everything on the diamond finesse, declarer should first try the extra chance that the ♣Q might be singleton or doubleton by playing the ♣A and a low club to dummy's ♣K. This gives declarer at least two chances, rather than one.

On the actual hand, North's ♣Q appears on the second round, so there's no need to risk the diamond finesse. Declarer can take the ♠Q and the rest of the club winners. If the ♣Q had not fallen, West could try the diamond finesse as a second chance. If North had shown out on the second round of clubs, declarer could safely lead toward the ♣J after taking the ♠Q, rather than taking the diamond finesse. Even if both opponents had followed with low clubs, declarer would still have the option of playing a third round of clubs rather than taking the diamond finesse. As long as South has the ♣Q, North can never get the lead.

Playing the ♣A and ♣K before deciding whether to take the diamond finesse gives declarer the best possible chance.

Defense

If South plays the ♥K on the first trick and continues with the ♥J, North must be careful to overtake with the ♥Q to continue leading the suit and establish the remaining hearts as winners.

HAND: 4-3
DEALER: SOUTH
VUL: E-W

NORTH
♠ K Q 7
♥ 10 7 6 4 3
♦ 8 7 4 2
♣ 9

WEST
♠ 8 6 3
♥ 9 2
♦ Q J 10 6
♣ A 5 4 3

EAST
♠ A 5
♥ A Q J
♦ A
♣ K Q J 10 7 6 2

SOUTH
♠ J 10 9 4 2
♥ K 8 5
♦ K 9 5 3
♣ 8

WEST	NORTH	EAST	SOUTH
			Pass
Pass	Pass	2♣	Pass
2♦	Pass	3♣	Pass
4♣	Pass	4NT	Pass
5♦	Pass	5NT	Pass
6♣	Pass	Pass	Pass

Bidding

East has only 21 high-card points, but the seven-card suit makes this hand worth a strong two-bid. East starts with the *artificial* opening bid of 2♣. West makes the *waiting response* of 2♦. Now East rebids 3♣ to show the club suit for the first time.

With a nice hand for clubs, West raises to 4♣. At this point, East might simply jump to 6♣, hoping to find enough in the West hand to make a slam. A more scientific approach is to use the *Blackwood convention*, bidding 4NT to ask how many aces West holds. If West were to show no aces by responding 5♣, East could always pass and play there. Instead, West responds 5♦, showing one ace. With the partnership holding all the aces, East might now try 5NT, asking about kings and looking for a grand slam. When West responds 6♣, showing no kings, East can settle for the small slam.

Opening Lead

Holding two kings against a slam contract, it would be dangerous to lead either suit, especially knowing that East-West have all the aces. A better choice is the ♠J, top of a sequence, hoping to get tricks with both the kings later in the play.

Play

The spade lead establishes a spade trick for the opponents and, at first glance, it may seem that declarer has to stake everything on a successful heart finesse . . . but there's a much safer play.

Declarer should take advantage of dummy's excellent diamonds. Declarer can establish two additional tricks in that suit to go along with the ♦A, by driving out the ♦K. Together with the ♠A, ♥A, and seven club tricks, that's 12 tricks in all. There are two challenges, however. Declarer must avoid losing a spade trick while driving out the ♦K, and declarer will need two entries to the dummy.

After winning the ♠A, declarer should play the ♣K to draw trump and then the ♦A. Next, declarer should lead a high club—*not the ♣2*—and overtake with dummy's ♣A. Now the ♦Q is led. If North were to play the ♦K, declarer could ruff with a high club and play the ♣2 over to dummy to take the established diamond winners, discarding the spade loser and a heart loser.

On the actual hand, North follows with a low diamond. Now declarer should *discard the spade loser.* This trick loses to South's ♦K, but that's the last trick for the defense. South can lead a spade, but East ruffs with a high club and leads the carefully preserved ♣2 over to dummy. The ♥J and ♥Q are discarded on dummy's two diamond winners and declarer makes the contract without risking the heart finesse. The technique of discarding the spade loser on the losing diamond trick is referred to as *discarding a loser on a loser.*

Defense

If declarer finds the winning line of play, there's nothing the defense can do . . . but it's more likely declarer will simply try the heart finesse.

HAND: 4-4
DEALER: WEST
VUL: BOTH

NORTH
♠ J 9 3
♥ J 5 2
♦ 8 6 4 2
♣ 7 6 3

WEST
♠ 7 5 4 2
♥ 7
♦ Q 10 7 3
♣ Q J 10 5

EAST
♠ 10 6
♥ Q 10 8 4
♦ K J
♣ K 9 8 4 2

SOUTH
♠ A K Q 8
♥ A K 9 6 3
♦ A 9 5
♣ A

WEST	NORTH	EAST	SOUTH
Pass	Pass	Pass	2♣
Pass	2♦	Pass	2♥
Pass	2NT	Pass	3♠
Pass	4♥	Pass	Pass
Pass			

Bidding

South opens with a strong artificial 2♣ bid and North makes a 2♦ waiting response. South shows the heart suit. This bid is forcing, just as if South opened with an old-fashioned strong 2♥ bid. Unless the partnership has another agreement, North bids 2NT to show a very weak hand—the same agreement that is commonly used when the partnership plays strong two-bids. If South were now to rebid only 3♥, most partnerships would allow North to pass with a really bad hand.

On the actual hand, South shows a second suit by bidding 3♠. With equal length in partner's suits, North *gives preference* back to 4♥. North can infer that South has more hearts than spades. With equal length, South would bid spades first. After the 4♥ bid, South has nothing more to say since North hasn't made any encouraging bids.

Opening Lead

Against 4♥, West starts with the ♣Q, top of the sequence.

Play

Declarer can afford three losers. There are two sure losers in the diamond suit, but none in spades or clubs. Declarer can afford to lose one trump trick, but not two. That will be easy if the missing hearts are divided 3-2, and declarer might make an overtrick if the ♥Q falls early.

Declarer should consider what might go wrong. A problem will arise only if the missing hearts are unfavorably divided. Declarer can't do much if they are divided 5-0, but can guard against a 4-1 break.

After winning the ♣A, declarer should play the ♥A and then *a low heart toward dummy*. On the actual hand, West discards on the second round of hearts and dummy's ♥J is used to force out East's ♥Q. East will likely play a club, which declarer ruffs. Knowing that East has two hearts remaining, declarer now plays the ♠8 to dummy's ♠J and leads the last heart from dummy. Declarer can finesse the ♥9 and then play the ♥K to draw East's last trump. Then declarer can safely take the remaining spade winners and ♦A to make the contract.

To appreciate why declarer should lead a low heart toward dummy's ♥J after playing the ♥A, suppose the East-West hearts were exchanged with West holding ♥Q-10-8-4. Now, whether West plays the ♥Q or a low heart, declarer will get a trick with dummy's ♥J and lose only one trump trick.

What if the missing hearts were divided 3-2 all along? Then, after the opponents win the second heart trick with the ♥Q, declarer still makes ten tricks after regaining the lead and drawing the last trump.

If declarer were to play the ♥A-K on this hand, the unfortunate heart division would mean that the defenders get two hearts to go along with their two diamond tricks to defeat the contract. Playing the ♥A and then a low heart toward the ♥J is called a *safety play* since it guarantees the contract even if the hearts are divided 4-1.

Defense

The defenders can't defeat the contract if declarer handles the heart suit carefully but should come out on top if declarer plays the ♥A-K.

Glossary

Artificial bid
A call during the auction which, by partnership agreement, carries a special message unrelated to the suit bid. For example, 2♣, a strong opening bid, doesn't necessarily show clubs.

Balanced Hand
A hand with no voids, no singletons, and at most one doubleton. There are only three balanced hand patterns: 4-3-3-3; 4-4-3-2; and 5-3-3-2. Borderline cases are 5-4-2-2 and 6-3-2-2.

Balance (Balancing)
Bidding when a pass would mean the opponents could buy the contract at a low level. 1♥—Pass—Pass to you.

Better Minor
Opening the bidding in the longer minor suit, or the stronger of two equal-length minor suits, when there is no five-card or longer major suit in the hand.

Bid
A number from 1 to 7, combined with a denomination: clubs, diamonds, hearts, spades, or notrump.

Call
Any bid, double, redouble, or pass.

Constructive Bid
A bid that suggests strength but is not forcing. An opening bid at the one-level is constructive.

Describer
Another term for the opener who gives a picture of the strength and shape of the hand to responder.

Distribution
The number of cards held in each suit in a player's hand. Points for distribution are added to the high-card points when valuing a hand.

Doubleton
A holding of two cards in a suit. A useless doubleton has no high cards.

Equal Vulnerability
When both sides are non vulnerable or both sides are vulnerable.

Favorable Vulnerability
When your side is non vulnerable and the opponents are vulnerable.

Five-card Majors
An agreement that an opening bid of 1♥ or 1♠ shows at least a five-card or longer suit.

First Position (Hand)
The dealer, who is the first player to have the chance to bid or pass.

Forcing Bid
A bid that partner is not expected to pass.

Fourth Position
The fourth player to have the chance to make a call. The player to the dealer's right.

Frozen Suit
A suit in which the side to first lead the suit sacrifices a trick.

High Cards
The top four cards in each suit: ace, king, queen, and jack.

High-Card Points (HCPs)
The point-count value given to the high cards in a hand: ace, 4; king, 3; queen, 2; jack, 1.

Hold Up
Letting the opponents win a trick that you could win.

Invitational Bid
A bid which encourages partner to continue bidding but doesn't insist on another bid.

Major Suit
Hearts or spades.

Minor Suit
Clubs or diamonds.

Non Vulnerable
A side, in rubber bridge, that has not won a game. The schedule of penalties for undertricks is not as steep as when vulnerable.

Obstructive Bid
A bid intended to interrupt the opponents' bidding conversation. A preempt.

Opener's rebid
Opener's second bid.

Pierson Points
See Rule of 15.

Penalty Double
A double made with the intention of increasing the bonus for defeating the opponents' contract.

Playing Tricks
The tricks expected to be won from a hand when the contract is played in a specified trump suit.

Preemptive Opening Bid
An opening bid in a suit at the two level or higher, showing a long suit and a weak hand.

Preference
Returning to the first suit that partner bid is called giving preference.

Quantitative
A natural, non forcing bid that limits the strength of the hand to a narrow range. After a 1NT opening a response of 2NT is quantitative showing 8 or 9 points. Opener could pass or bid on.

Rule of 15
In borderline cases in fourth position, high-card points are added to the number of spades in the hand. If the total is 15 or more, the suggestion is to open the bidding. Otherwise, pass.

Rule of 20
In borderline cases in first or second position, the high-card points are added to the number of cards in the two longest suits. If the total is 20 or more, the suggestion is to open the bidding. Otherwise pass.

Rule of 500
Overbidding by two tricks when vulnerable and three tricks when non vulnerable to avoid going down more than 500 points even if doubled.

Second Position (Hand)
The player to the left of the dealer.

Short Club
An opening bid of 1♣ with fewer than four cards in the suit. Frequently used when the hand has no five-card or longer major suit.

Singleton
A holding of one card in a suit.

Solid Sequence
Three or more consecutive cards in a suit, headed by an honor.

Strong Two-bid
An opening bid in a suit at the two level that is forcing to the game level.

Third Position
The partner of the dealer.

Unbalanced
A hand with a void, a singleton, or more than one doubleton.

Unblock
Play or discard high cards in a suit from one hand to gain advantage in the opposite hand.

Unfavorable Vulnerability
When your side is vulnerable and the opponents are non vulnerable.

Void
A holding of zero cards in a suit

Vulnerable
A side, in rubber bridge, that has won a game. The schedule of penalties for undertricks is steeper than when non vulnerable.

Weak Two-bid
An opening bid at the two level in a suit, showing a six-card suit and about 5-11 high-card points.

Let's keep in touch.
Visit my website:

www.BetterBridge.com
www.AudreyGrant.com

or send an E-mail to:

BetterBridge@home.com

Festivals with Audrey Grant
contact:

Dawson's Bridge Vacations

P.O. Box 186
Reading, MA 01867

1-800-942-6119